A Story of Books and Libraries

by

ALICE DAMON RIDER

The Scarecrow Press, Inc.
Metuchen, N.J.   1976

Library of Congress Cataloging in Publication Data

Rider, Alice Damon, 1895-
    A story of books and libraries.

    Includes bibliographies and index.
    1. Books--History. 2. Libraries--History. 3. Writ-
ing--History. I. Title.
Z4.R535   001.55'2   76-7596
ISBN 0-8108-0930-3

"Mine is yesterday.   I know tomorrow."

--The Book of the Dead,
3000 B. C.

CONTENTS

PREFACE

This handbook is designed for use in the Arts, Social Sciences and Humanities courses in high schools.

The chapters in the handbook may be used as:

An affirmation in this day of "media culture" of the role of the book in understanding and interpreting man's achievements and best thinking, whether recorded on stone, clay, papyrus, parchment or paper.

An introduction to broad fields of exploration and research for students involved in self learning and independent study.

A supplementary source, offered by the projects suggested at the end of each chapter, to enrich units of work and to create new and imaginative approaches to art, music, social studies and literature.

Suggestions for the teacher who realizes the interrelationship of books and libraries with man's progress through the ages, and who integrates this theme with subject disciplines.

A source book for the librarian in developing with teachers an appreciation of books and libraries.

And finally, this handbook is for the imaginative student determined to seek beyond the covers of his textbook ever-widening horizons for his or her professional future. The medium may not be the message, but there is "magic in the book."

This handbook has been in preparation for many years, inspired by the contributions of a host of students in college classes.

It is dedicated with respect and affection to my sister, Florence Damon Cleary, Professor Emeritus, Wayne State University, Detroit, Michigan.

Alice Damon Rider
Professor Emeritus
State University College
  of Arts and Sciences
Geneseo, New York

March, 1975

Chapter 1

MAN'S EARLIEST RECORDS

"There is no past so long
as books shall live. "
--Edward Bulwer-Lytton

An ancient hand print on a cave wall proclaimed, "I am man. " The incessant print-out of a computer in the modern world is an unbroken link with that hand print. Both attest to man's struggle since prehistory to communicate both orally and in writing his thoughts, his ideas, his triumphs, his defeats, whether they related to the hammering out of a flint head, the building of the Pyramids or the plotting of a moon shot.

THE ORAL TRADITION

Long before the written word, man began his record keeping with oral communication. The cries, grunts and squeals which have long been accepted as the genesis of speech in men of prehistory, led to slowly developing speech patterns in which experiences were recounted and passed by word of mouth from generation to generation--the oral tradition.

Story Telling

Story telling, the oldest of the arts, is man's earliest attempt to communicate and to perpetuate his rituals and folk lore. In the market place of an ancient city, a grizzled tribesman told stories of the creation of the world, the gods, great floods and endless wars. A Medicine Man by a camp

1

fire recounted tales of hunting trips, the "big snow," the ambush and torture of a mighty warrior.

Wandering minstrels sang of Ulysses; of Apollo who drove the chariot, Sun; of Thor and his hammer; of Pluto's capture of Persephone, whose yearly return to Earth became the symbol of spring; of Perseus and the slaying of the Gorgon, Medusa. Man used stories to explain wonders he may not have understood, but wished to remember.

Did your family keep traditions alive by story telling? On cold, snowy nights, Grandfather lay on the floor beside a red-hot, pot-bellied stove, his head resting on a chunk of wood, and told his wide-eyed grandchildren tales of Indian braves, witches and their spells, early settlers building their log houses, torch light parades on election nights, and a bitter morning when he found in his Christmas stocking nothing but a raw potato.

Tales of the Origin of Writing

To the gods were attributed strange tales, told and retold, explaining the origin of writing. The Chinese believed that a four-eyed dragon man saw patterns in the stars and from them created written characters. The god Thoth, who had the head of a bird, was said to have originated Egyptian hieroglyphs, or "sacred writing." In India, the god Brahma conceived the forms of writing from a study of the seams in the human skull. The Greek myth about writing concerns Cadmus and the "sowing of the dragon's teeth"--the teeth being the 16 letters of an alphabet brought to Greece from Phoenicia.

These myths and legends, whether told by a tribal elder around a camp fire or in a market place by a story teller, are believed to be an explanation of the unknown and to have been passed from generation to generation as a part of the oral tradition.

MNEMONIC DEVICES

Older than written symbols are mnemonic or memory devices--a means of silent communication.

Notched or tally sticks, an early form of memory device, were commonly used to register the passing of days, a count of the flocks or the amount of harvested grains. One immediately remembers Robinson Crusoe who, as a castaway, used a notched or tally stick to record each passing day; or Billy the Kid, who boasted of 21 notches on his gun.

Not long ago, aborigines, living in the Australian bush, used tally sticks to send messages. Two notches in a stock signified that a certain number of men or women were needed for a raiding party or for a peaceful harvest. Three notches may have denoted a time span. Usually the memory stick was carried by a messenger as a reminder of a message he was to deliver.

It was discovered, however, that a knotted cord was a better memory device than a notched tally stick, since the knots could be untied and the cord used again. Hanging at various intervals from a main cord were bunches of knotted cords. The knots, of different types, were secured in certain positions on the main cord and represented numbers relative to population, taxes, flocks and an amazing variety of other essential records. Knot keepers were present in each village to tie and to interpret the meaning of the knots.

A story is told of the mighty King Darius who left with his soldiers a cord tied into 60 knots. A knot was to be untied each day, and if the King had not returned when the last knot was untied, the men were to go home. History doesn't tell whether or not the 60th knot was untied.

From China to the land of the Incas the knotted strings were used to keep careful records. Not even the Spanish conquerors dared to disturb this record-keeping of the Incas. It must have been a highly workable system as it controlled a wondrous people who did not know how to write. The knotted cords were known as Quipu, the Indian name for knot.

These symbols of protowriting--the notched or tally stick and the knotted cord--were common for centuries before writing, and with other mnemonic devices of various forms, they are still in use today.

Wampum

Wampum was used by the North American Indian for ornament, ceremonial pledges and money. Polished shells and bird bones, white or dyed purple, were strung in strands, belts and sashes. A Treaty Belt given to William Penn is an example of the commemorative use of wampum as a mnemonic device.

A Catalog of Mnemonic Devices

Serving as unspoken words assisting the memory, mnemonic devices surround us today--road signs, a barber pole, stop and go lights, a cross, a string around the finger, a flag, notches in an outlaw's gun, a peace pipe, a V for victory, chessmen and punctuation marks. It is possible to collect a most extensive list of these devices which are very much a part of everyday life.

The oral tradition and mnemonic devices prefaced man's greatest invention: the written word.

THE MAKING OF AN ALPHABET

If one believes that whatever is to come cannot out-weigh the importance to man of what has gone before, then the art of writing, which recorded and preserved the past, is man's most generous gift to man.

With writing, man became civilized. It is not un-usual, however, when the history of this art is explored, to limit its beginnings to the alphabet, and particularly to our ABC's. Forty-nine other alphabets are in use in the world today and scholars state that in the development of the writ-ten word, 200 different alphabets have been used.

A Preview: From Z Backwards

If not with the 26 letters, how and where did writing develop?

Until other archeological "finds" are unearthed and deciphered, scholars generally agree that man began to write

about 5000 B.C., 35,000 years after he learned to speak.
As far back as the Stone Age, scratches on bone, tally sticks
and knotted cords, known as proto-writing, were used to record ownership and to communicate beyond the range of the
human voice.

Writing is a means of communication dependent upon
common signs that are sent, received and understood. Hence
it was with pictures in sequence, indicating the spoken word,
that writing began. Pictographic writing helped man to organize his life, and in turn, an organized society led to the
spread of writing. With the birth of the written word came
recorded history.

It is probable that between 3000 and 1000 B.C. writing evolved simultaneously in several unrelated places. One
scholar claims that writing was invented six different times.
Sumerian cuneiform and Egyptian hieroglyphic symbols were
devised concurrently.

However, not until the seafaring Phoenicians needed
simple records for trading with the Egyptians in the mines
of the Sinai Peninsula was there a hint of alphabetic symbols.
In 1904, Sir Flinders Petrie, a distinguished Egyptologist,
discovered near the mines in Sinai, stones inscribed with
symbols, 25 of which have been identified as truly alphabetic.

The Phoenicians, living in the melting pot of Eastern
tribes, were so named by Homer in the Iliad. They were
undoubtedly responsible for the development of an alphabet
consisting only of consonants.

The Greeks borrowed the consonants, added the vowels
and passed their "Western" alphabet to Rome. Along the way,
many alphabets spun off, ours, after additions and subtrac-
tions, coming from Rome.

To understand the various alphabetic and non-alphabetic
writings, it was necessary to translate the symbols; only
then could the story of civilization be told.

Scholars have discovered the keys that unlock several
early scripts. The Frenchman Champollion opened up the
story of the glorious civilization of ancient Egypt with the
translation of the hieroglyphic writing. Henry Rawlinson, an
English archeologist, deciphered a trilingual cuneiform inscription carved on a cliff during the reign of Darius the

Great. Rawlinson's key to cuneiform made it possible in 1967 to translate a letter written 30 centuries ago in the city of Ur. Cretan writing, invented about 2000 B.C., was deciphered only as recently as 1952. Now scholars can spill gallons of ink in arguments as to whether the fabled city of Minos, on the island of Crete, was a cemetery or a magnificent center of a wondrous culture.

In summary, and with the reservation that an archeologist, digging in the ruins of an ancient city, may upset this time chart, here is a brief chronology of early writing:

40,000 B.C.	Man speaks
30,000 B.C.	Cave drawings
20,000 B.C.	Tallies on sticks, bones and cords
3,000 B.C.	Pictographic symbols
3,000 B.C.	Hieroglyphs
3,000 B.C.	Cuneiform symbols
1400-800 B.C.	Alphabetic symbols

It does not greatly matter who drew the first symbols. The evolution of writing followed a common pattern based on five developmental steps, overlapping and leaning on other systems of written symbols, but maintaining an over-all constant progression.

Five Steps to an Alphabet

The five steps are: 1) the pictograph, 2) the ideogram, 3) the phonogram, 4) the syllabic sound symbols, and 5) the letter sound symbols.

Step 1. The Pictograph: The "Thing" Picture. In the shadowy past, as man struggled to communicate by written language, lies the unsolved mystery of the meaning of a multitude of rude pictures on bones, potsherds (clay vessels) and cave walls. Archeologists continue to excavate sites and study the findings, only to admit that the artifacts of prehistory baffle them. An immense period of prehistory is lost.

Recent studies have placed the origin of man in the valley of the River Omo in Ethiopia four million years ago. However, rich archeological finds have led some scholars to call France the capital of prehistory. In the fertile valley surrounding Dordogne, layer after layer of rocks tell the story of the Neanderthal and Cro-Magnon cave men, who attempted from 400,000 B. C. to 10,000 B. C. to express themselves in written symbols. Now under study at Harvard University is a piece of bone, tentatively dated 400,000 B. C., carved with four parallel lines. Obviously the lines had been cut with flints, shaped by a bone hammer.

Uncovered on cave walls at Dordogne and Lascaux are fabulous drawings of bison in red and black, painted and modeled. The woolly mammoth, the giant elk, extinct since 20,000 B. C., and a bird perched on a stick are drawn with amazing skill. No acceptable theory has been advanced as to what these symbols represent. Were they records of hunting trips? Did they symbolize religious rituals? Were they an effort to portray a male and female society? Were the drawings a part of the initiation of a young hunter, giving him a sense of power by acquainting him with a picture of the animal he must kill if he would live? Why were these drawings on the walls of dark, secret caves rather than in caves in which man lived? Assuredly, the symbols reflected a thought process and were a form of written communication.

Similar to the cave paintings at Dordogne were those in the caves at Altamira, Spain. This archeological find was made by a man and his small daughter who wandered, by chance, into a cave. Huge bulls glared down at them from painted walls. The drawings may have been a record of a hunting trip, but there is probably some deeper meaning to the symbols.

One fact appears constant: written communication began with pictures, whether painted on cave walls, carved on bone by the Eskimos, drawn on cliff sides by American Indians, or formed on bones, rocks and potsherds gathered at the turn of the century by Sir Flinders Petrie from the area surrounding the Mediterranean Sea.

In early cave paintings a bison represented a bison; a bull, a bull; a deer, a deer. The painter merely said, "This is a bison, a bull or a deer."

Then a series of pictures or a picture story represented animals in action. Deer fought each other. Bison ran. Human figures were added and a picture story might depict hunters on a long journey after food, or warriors on a raiding party.

Later, picture stories developed into a rebus, a combination of symbols expressing an idea. For example, the drawing of a man and a stick-like cane signified an old man;

a man with a spear, a hunter. Ten short, vertical lines
under a picture of a deer denoted the number of animals
killed.

It was but a short step from the rebus to the ideogram.

Step 2. The Ideogram: The "Idea" Picture. Picto-
graphs as a form of writing were simple and concrete. However, when man wished to express an emotion or an abstrac-
tion such as courage, love or the hereafter, it was necessary
to present "thing" pictures in a more elaborate form--the
ideogram.

For example, in Egyptian ideographic writing a picture of an eagle meant, at first, just an eagle. Give the
eagle the face of a man and the idea of a godhead or the
soul of a man was now apparent. The symbol for water
joined with the symbol for mouth denoted thirst. Combining
the written symbols for eye and for water signified crying.

The stages of ideographic writing were fluid ones and
were easily misinterpreted. Did pictures of the sun and
moon side by side mean day or night or did they symbolize
an eclipse? Did a picture of man running mean he was es-
caping from danger or was on the war path--a man of courage or a coward?

Chinese writing is largely ideographic, using hundreds
of characters in combination; it is a very difficult language
to record and hence is held in reverence by the Chinese.

Step 3. The Phonogram: The "Sound" Picture. The
phonogram was developed by the use of the acrophonic principle. What is the acrophonic principle? The symbol is
named after the first sound of the word for which the symbol stands.

The Egyptian symbol for water was ᨆᨆ . Water
was called nu. Therefore the symbol ᨆᨆ was named N.

The symbol for mouth was ⌒. In Egyptian language ro was the symbol for mouth. ⌒ represented R.

⅄ stood as the symbol for ox in Phoenician. An
ox was called an aleph. The symbol was named A.

The naming of the symbol was a step nearer the alphabet. Then came a dramatic change in the form of the symbol. The eagle with a man's head had developed into a simple, easy-to-write symbol like this: $\mathcal{U}$

Step 4. A "Syllabic Sound" Picture. The cuneiform writing of the Sumerians, Babylonians and Assyrians was not alphabetic, like ours; it consisted of syllabic sound symbols-- a syllabary--bi, ab, bu, for example.

It is not surprising that this syllabic writing was of little interest to the Phoenicians. Syllabic sound pictures were awkward and complex.

Step 5. Letter Sound Pictures. This step marked the emergence of our alphabet. Centuries passed in the development from pictures to ideograms to phonograms to syllabic symbols and finally to letter names. There is no time chart for the clear-cut emergence of each step. But a logical progression was evident as, by trade and by war, man learned from men, adapting each development to his own needs.

MAN'S EARLY WRITTEN LANGUAGE

In several of the early cultures, writing never did progress through all of the five basic steps we have mentioned. With this fact in mind, note the development in Mesopotamian, Egyptian and Phoenician writing.

The Sumerians, Babylonians and Assyrians Write

Advancing from a picture to a syllabic script, cuneiform writing was, about 5000 B.C., an expression of the early culture of the Sumerians. They wrote on clay, the most readily available material, using a stylus which produced a wedge-shaped mark. Thus cuneiform writing received its name from the Latin word cuneus (wedge).

Archeological finds testify to the pictorial beginnings of cuneiform--a clay tablet uncovered at Uruk; the Hoffman tablet, a four-inch-square black stone dated 6000 B.C.; and small stone slabs, the Monuments Blau, dated 5000 B.C. and now preserved in the British Museum, London.

Cuneiform writing moved with history from the Sumerians to the Akkadians, who used 500 different phonetic symbols, and then to the Assyrians and on to the Babylonians. With the fall of Babylon, cuneiform was supposedly replaced by Aramaic. However, cuneiform writing persisted until the birth of Christ; it was second in the extent of its use only to Phoenician and Greek alphabetic writing.

Unlike the ornamental hieroglyphs of contemporary Egyptian writing, cuneiform was a practical every-day writing. For years scholars despaired of finding a key to the symbols. However, from a declaration of Darius the Great, carved on a cliff side (the Rock of Behistun), repeated symbols were recognized largely from the names of Kings. Cuneiform writing was unlocked. Ancient history can now be more accurately interpreted.

The Egyptians Write

Three thousand different hieroglyphs were drawn by the Egyptians, 300 being commonly used. Based on pictures of birds and animals, the written symbols or hieroglyphs were, at first, the prerogative of the priests. Hence came the term "sacred writing."

The Development of the Hieroglyph. Hieroglyphs were "thing" pictures. For example, the hieroglyph for scribe was a picture of a scribe with a sheet of writing material (papyrus) spread before him, in his hand a reed pen. Over each ear was a pen, one for red ink, one for black.

This picture writing appeared simple. However, the Egyptians did not "spell" anything the same way every time, and often used four or five different hieroglyphs for the same message.

The next step in the development of Egyptian writing, the ideogram or "idea" picture, was retained for centuries out of respect for things ancient. With conventional characters so perfectly written that they must have been used for centuries, the Send Inscription on stone, dated 4000 B.C., is an example of the regard for the long use of the basic symbols. The Inscription is preserved in a museum at Oxford University, England.

A change to phonograms (sound pictures) was slow

and confused. As many as 30 symbols for the sound of A
were indicative of the fact that a true alphabet never com-
pletely emerged, although in a final stage the letter sound
symbols were cut to 25. To these letter sounds were added
pictures which changed the meaning of the symbols, and often
led to confusion.

With trade and industry growing, a shortened form of
hieroglyphs was developed for the keeping of records. This
was the hieratic script used for all writing except inscriptions on monuments. A scribe, by holding his reed pen at
a new angle, found he could write the hieratic script more
rapidly and could join the symbols without lifting the pen from
the papyrus.

This was the script that the Phoenicians borrowed and
further simplified as they traded with the Egyptians, who
were mining in the Sinai Peninsula. A demotic script, which
emerged later, was little used.

The Decipherment of Hieroglyphic Writing. Hieroglyphic writing was not deciphered until Napoleon and his
soldiers conquered Egypt. The buried temples and tombs
had kept their silent secrets.

Quite by accident one of Napoleon's soldiers found,
sticking out of the sand near the village of Rosetta in Egypt,
a slab of black basalt four feet long. The soldier, realizing
that symbols were carved on the stone, took it to his com-
manding officer, who in turn delivered it to Napoleon. Recognizing Greek writing on the stone, Napoleon ordered it to be
kept in Cairo for study.

When Napoleon was forced to retreat from Egypt and
a treaty was signed, one clause of the treaty gave the Rosetta
Stone to the English. The Stone was put on display at the
British Museum. Perfectly mounted, it is one of England's
great treasures.

What of the decipherment of the symbols on the Rosetta Stone? It was determined that lines of three different
scripts had been carved on the stone--hieroglyphic, demotic
and Greek. The Greek could be read and scholars judged,
hopefully, that the other scripts repeated the contents of the
Greek inscription. The theory proved to be correct.

Champollion, a French scholar, believed that cartouches

(ovals) in the hieroglyphic script contained the names of Cleopatra and Ptolemy. Working on this premise, Champollion translated several symbols, adding meanwhile a third name, Alexander, as a key word. Before his death, Champollion had succeeded in translating the hieroglyphic writing, thus opening to the world the magnificence of the early Egyptian culture.

The Phoenicians Write

In ships 70 feet long, equipped with purple sails, the Phoenicians, an adventuresome people, may have sailed around Africa 2000 years before European explorers attempted the lengthy sea voyage. Clad in crimson clothes, the Phoenician seamen worried not about a flat world, culminating in a vast chasm, but sailed their trading ships into Mediterranean ports and beyond the Gates of Hercules.

A nation of traders and business men, the Phoenicians were for a time under the domination of Egypt. In 1200 B. C. they won independence only to be conquered by the Babylonians, the Assyrians and Persians and, finally, the Macedonians. In the conquest of Phoenicia, the soldiers of Alexander the Great killed and enslaved 38, 000 Phoenicians.

But the Phoenicians continued to trade. Cargoes of ivory, tin, spices, perfumes, weapons, jewelry, papyrus, glass and crimson-dyed cloth were loaded on ships, sailing from the city of Byblos, the famous port of trade on the Mediterranean. Byblos, translated later in the Greek language, became biblos, meaning book. From its roots came our word Bible.

The Phoenicians Borrow a Script. Egypt was the favored country for Phoenician commerce, largely because of the iron mines in the Sinai Peninsula. An accounting system was essential in this exchange of trade. But the Egyptian hieratic script was too cumbersome for the lively Phoenicians. Simple, quickly drawn symbols emerged in the recording of business transactions--the first faint stirrings of letter sound symbols.

The distinguished scholars, Sir Flinders Petrie and Martin Sprengling were, however, cautious in accepting the hieratic script as the only source of the Phoenician alphabet. Undoubtedly the Phoenicians traded with the Babylonians and Assyrians and knew the cuneiform symbols.

It was also probable that Phoenician sailors had marveled at the glory of Cretan culture as they sailed into the bays of that island. Palaces, factories, temples, jewels, statues and written records testified to a wondrous civilization that later mysteriously vanished. Cretan writing, found in 1900 by archeologists in the city of King Minos was deciphered in 1952. Scholars now have a "Cretan Rosetta Stone."

As intelligent borrowers, the Phoenicians may have incorporated ideas from several scripts, arriving finally at 22 basic characters, all consonants, with alphabetic sounds derived by the application of the acrophonic principle--the name of the letter is the first sound of the word for which the letter stands. Their writing was practical and concerned with day-to-day business affairs. They wrote on papyrus, a perishable material. They left no papyrus rolls, no literature and only a few inscriptions.

Phoenician Inscriptions. Fifty years ago the Ahiram Inscription was uncovered. Carved over the door of the tomb of Ahiram, King of Byblos in 1250 B.C., was a curse placed there by his son to protect the body of his father. A sample of several letters in the Inscription follows:

﬩ﬤ9ﬡﬥ3ﬦﬧ'39ﬨﬧ9ﬥ.

The Inscription read from right to left. With imagination one might recognize a possible beginning of an alphabet. The short stroke ﬡ is not a letter, but is used to separate words.

Found in the ruins of a Phoenician colony on the island of Cyprus and decorated with letters around the lip was a bronze bowl dated roughly 1000 B.C. One of the letters on the bowl was an ⊀ , an A turned sideways.

Discovered near the Dead Sea, and now housed at the Louvre in Paris, was the Moabite Stone, inscribed 892 B.C. The Stone bears the record of a great rebellion of the Moabites against the Israelites. The Arabs on whose land the stone was found were loath to let it fall into Christian hands. Water was poured over the Stone and a fire built around it. The Stone shattered. The patched Stone is a memorable relic of a Phoenician alphabet.

When the Phoenician traders from Tyre carried their alphabet of 22 consonants to Greece about 900 B.C., it was one of the most important voyages in the history of civilization.

The Greeks Write

The early Greeks, living in the city-states of Athens, Sparta and Corinth, gloried in the wondrous tales of the blind Homer and in the Golden Age of Pericles. In spite of wars between the city-states, the arts, including literature and writing, flourished and were enjoyed by all the Greeks.

The Source of Greek Letters. Most scholars agree that writing came to Greece from Phoenicia about 900 B.C. From the seaports of Phoenicia, trading ships sailed in and out of the Aegean Isles. Undoubtedly Phoenician letters were used in commercial transactions and the curious Greeks might well have wondered about this mysterious form of communication, then freely adopted it.

The historian Herodotus told of a company of Phoenicians, led by the hero, Cadmus, who came to Thera and sowed the "dragon's teeth"--probably the Phoenician letters. Interestingly enough, the oldest form of Greek writing was found in Thera.

The Greek Contribution to Writing. The early Greeks wrote the Phoenician letters in any fashion they pleased. However, by 650 B.C. according to the Gortyna Inscription, the letters were clear and beautifully proportioned. The *ᴎ* of the Phoenicians became a Grecian M.

The Phoenicians wrote from right to left, the Greeks from left to right. A very strange writing style was, for a time, popular, but was abandoned because of its complexity. Known as boustrophedon (oxen plowing), it went in and out like a giant S, or began in the center and widened into a circle.

To the 22 consonants used by the Phoenicians, the Greeks added vowels; these at first denoted breathings in speech. Sentences did not begin with capital letters nor was there spacing between words, but some use was made of punctuation and paragraphing.

The Greeks named their letters A, B, etc, not by a single sound as we do, but by a word--alpha, beta, kappa, lambda, psi. From the names of A, alpha, and B, beta, came the word alphabet.

As many as ten different alphabets developed in Greece.

The "Eastern" alphabet moved to the Slavic countries, the "Western" alphabet to the Romans and thence to us.

The Romans Write

The Etruscans, their origin in hidden history, were by 1100 B.C. a flourishing colony north of Rome. They built magnificent temples, cast pottery, designed jewelry and--judging from tomb inscriptions--used an alphabet. The letters were early Greek, but are thus far undecipherable.

An ivory writing tablet, the Marsalina Tablet, dated 700 B.C. and coated with wax for a writing surface, bears evidence of an alphabet of 25 letters. The tablet was probably a child's copy book. A translation baffles scholars.

For 500 years, the Etruscans and Romans fought each other in an attempt to control Italy. In 281 B.C., the Romans were the conquerors but were greatly influenced by the religion, laws and arts of the conquered. It is likely that Roman scholars understood Etruscan writing and examined it with care.

The Greeks and Romans may have worked simultaneously on an alphabet, even to experimenting on the boustrophedon manner of writing.

As Rome rose to power, forays into Greece became numerous and Greek scholar-slaves, libraries and papyrus rolls were eagerly seized as spoils of war and brought to Rome.

The Roman Alphabet. The Romans were practical people and reduced the conglomeration of alphabets--Etruscan and Greek--to clear, easily read letters.

Roman accomplishments in the making of an alphabet were distinctive.

The Romans named the letters by a single sound, instead of a word as used by the Greeks. For example, A for alpha, B for beta.

The Greek alphabets were reduced by the Romans to 23 letters: A B E Z H I K M N O T X Y C G L S P R D V F Q. The letter Z was not used at first, and when

it was restored it was placed at the end of the alphabet.
Note also that the letters J U W were not a part of the
Roman alphabet; they were added in medieval times.
The Greeks seldom used Q, but the Romans did.   A
second letter, V, followed Q as an aid to pronunciation.
Q seldom stands without U (V) in our language.

As important as these contributions were, they were
minimized by the great Roman capitals--crisp, clear
and still used as models for capitals in the art of let-
tering.

The Roman Capitals.   Until the Christian era, the
Romans used only great capital letters.   The beauty of the
letters depended on a perfect balance of thick and thin strokes
as well as the weight of the letter at the base due to the
serifs or finishing strokes.   The most impressive capital
letters (majuscules) were the Monumental or Square capitals
--so perfect in form that each appeared to be drawn with a
compass and ruler.

The capitals were chiseled on stone with a graver.
On papyrus a double-edged tool resembling two pens bound
together was used.

Three types of these magnificent majuscules were:
Square, already described, Rustic and Uncial.   A comparison of the letter a in the three types can be made from
these examples:

Square   Rustic   Uncial

The Rustic capitals, with smaller serifs and with
horizontal lines drawn heavier than vertical lines, could be
joined or written cursively, and hence could be written much
more rapidly.

The word uncial means "inch," and the smaller,
rounded uncial capitals permitted even greater speed in writing.   Uncials were usually reserved for the copying of early

Christian writings.   Pagan literature was written in Square
or Rustic capitals.

The Roman alphabet and the Latin language spread
via wars and colonization to the peoples of Europe.   Changes
were made in the script (form of writing) but few changes
were made in the alphabet--even to this day.

WRITING IN MEDIEVAL TIMES

It is said that St. Patrick taught the Celtic monks to
write the Square, Rustic and Uncial capital letters of the
Romans.   To save time and to conserve parchment, the monks
refined the Roman uncials into more rounded and more graceful forms.   For example, E became Є , D became ᗪ.   A
few minuscule or lower case letters, known as semi-uncial,
crept into the writing.   One of the most beautiful books in the
world--the Book of Kells--was copied in semi- or half-uncial
script.

It was the scholar, Alcuin, who introduced the carefully selected minuscules, or small letters, to the monks
copying in the Scriptoria of the Carolingian monasteries.
Writing now became a blend of capitals and lower case (or
small) letters.

In the 12th century, the high-shouldered, pointed,
black-letter Gothic script appeared.   It was supposedly pat-
terned on the pointed arches of the Gothic cathedrals.   A
"pretty" script, Gothic was difficult to read and very difficult to write.

NATIONAL HANDS

As European nations assumed identity, writing was no
longer in Latin, but in the vernacular, the language of the individual country.   Scripts varied greatly and were burdened
with countless abbreviations of words and with fancy letters.
One script, almost impossible to read, resorted to the ex-
ceedingly long ascenders and descenders--that is, very long
upward or downward strokes on letters like p or h.

With the coming of the Renaissance, a clear, rounded,

easily read script, the Humanistic, was developed. Early
printers, who had struggled to cut type faces in Gothic,
turned gladly to the use of the Humanistic as a model for
their type.   You are now reading a printed page based on
Humanistic script.

In the next 50 years intricate electronic letter making
may alter our written symbols--no less an amazing change
in written communication than the change from the great
painted bulls on the cave walls at Altamira to the printing
press of Johann Gutenberg.

THE ART OF WRITING: A REVIEW

Man's heroes, his gods, his explanations of the phe-
nomena of nature, his hunting trips, his conquests in battle
were perpetuated in tales, myths and legends passed by word
of mouth from one generation to another.

Man recorded also the changes of seasons, noted the
passing of days, counted his flocks and remembered events
by the use of mnemonic devices--unspoken words.

From cave drawings of prehistory to the machines of
modern communication, man has used 200 alphabets and has
created numberless scripts in a desire to leave records of
his culture.

Westward from Rome through Europe the alphabet became a part of our heritage.   To be remembered were the
Sumerians, Babylonians, Cretans, Egyptians, Phoenicians,
Etruscans and Greeks who borrowed written symbols from
each other, changing and adapting them to the specific needs
of their cultures, until by commerce and conquest the varied
symbols were formed by the Romans into an alphabet.

Inscriptions, deciphered by scholars, unlocked the
secrets of ancient writings--the Rock of Behistun, the key to
cuneiform; the Rosetta Stone to hieroglyphics; the Moabite
Stone to alphabetic writing.

Out of the great Square capitals, the "arty" Rustics,
the inch-high, rounded Uncials, the minuscules (small letters), a variety of scripts developed to include the Humanistic,
a model for much of our present day printing.

To review the art of writing is to review the history of man. Writing mirrors the past, records for the future and lives in the present.

"PRACTICE MAKES PERFECT"

You are responsible for the posting of notices in school corridors regarding a presentation of Fiddler on the Roof by the Drama Club. Why not write the notices in boustrophedon, a Greek writing style?

Select a word such as Manuscript and on a 4" x 12" bristol board, write the word Manuscript in Square, Rustic and Uncial capital letters. Use the idea for an art project. Paste on the back of the board a paper bearing a brief description of early Roman writing. A book entitled The 26 Letters, by Oscar Ogg, will be of help to you in this project.

When the next research paper or an oral class room presentation is assigned to you, try using the material in this chapter as a starting point. Consider these topics:

The Phoenicians - An Unusual People

Dr. Leakey's Six Million Year Old Man

The Rosetta Stone and Its Secret

Do you know the traditions and folklore of your family? A discussion of this subject at home may lead to the fashioning of a Jesse tree (a family genealogy) or an investigation of local folklore.

Graphology is the science of analyzing character traits by means of handwriting. Many books have been written on the subject. You might be interested to know what a decided backward of forward slant in your handwriting tells about you as a person.

FURTHER READING

Claiborne, Robert. The Birth of Writing. New York: Time-

Life Books, c. 1974.
"Among all the revolutionary creations of man, writing ranks as the supreme intellectual achievement." From these first words of the Introduction to the final pages of a flow chart on the Emergence of Man, the history of writing is made a part of man's mysterious past. Far from a picture book, although there is a highly knowledgeable picture on every page, many in color.

Diringer, David. The Alphabet: A Key to the History of Mankind. 3rd ed. rev. New York: Funk and Wagnalls, 1968.
For the more mature reader who wants a detailed and precise account of the development of writing. Illustrated.

Marek, Kurt (C. W. Ceram, pseud.). Gods, Graves and Scholars. New York: Knopf, 1964.
Excitement and adventure to be found in the mystery of "diggings." In your school and public library are many fascinating books on archeology. Check out Four Thousand Years Ago by Geoffrey Bibby; Leonard Cottrell's Digs and Diggers; and Ancient Ruins and Archeology by the DeCamps.

Ogg, Oscar. The 26 Letters. rev. ed. New York: Crowell, 1971.
Extraordinarily clear and simple line drawings in brown and black tell the story of the alphabet in this easy-to-read book.

Chapter 2

FROM STONES TO PRINT-OUTS

"There is always another window. "
--Ogden Nash

The materials upon which man wrote determined to a large extent his manner of writing. Many times and in many different ways this idea was illustrated.

Through the ages man has written on bone, on rocks attached and detached, on animal skins, tree bark, silk and linen cloth, wood, bamboo, bronze and pottery. These materials altered the shape of the written symbols and the actual form of the "book. "

However, clay, papyrus, parchment and paper have, for centuries, been indispensable writing materials, and more symbols have been written on these materials than all others combined.

"THEY WROTE ON CLAY"

Literally tons of Mesopotamian clay tablets have been unearthed--tablets made of river mud (clay). The tablets varied in size and shape--square, round and oblong with rounded corners. Usually the tablets were flat on top and slightly rounded on the bottom.

The scribe used as a writing instrument a thin, pencil-like piece of wood cut diagonally on one end. Held tightly in the fist of the scribe, the stick was thrust into the wet clay where it formed wedge-shaped characters such as

▼▶✦. The writing instrument was called a cuneus
(wedge) and the characters cuneiform.

The tablets were then baked in the sun or in a kiln.
In an almost magical fashion, clay envelopes were made for
important documents. How these clay envelopes were con-
structed so that they did not adhere to the inner tablet is
still a question which cannot be answered.

A clay "book" was comprised of a series of tablets.
One might hazard a guess as to how many clay tablets would
be necessary to write a Tom Sawyer. In Chapter 3 the care
and arrangement of tablets in libraries are described.

In Ninevah, the capital of Babylonia, 30,000 clay tablets were uncovered by archeologists. Perhaps one day you
will be lucky enough to be able to examine some of the
20,000 clay tablets preserved in the British Museum, London.

A REED BY THE RIVER NILE

The papyrus reed grew along the fertile banks of the
Nile in Egypt. The plant was used for fuel and for making
rope. It was cooked and juiced for food, and was made into robes and sandals and fashioned into rafts and boats. Did
the Egyptians sail to America in papyrus boats centuries before Christopher Columbus made his historic journey?

The tall papyrus reed had a stalk as thick as a man's
wrist, spreading into a feathery top. It was first used as
writing material in Egypt and became a rich commercial re-
source as the demand for it grew in the countries around the
Mediterranean Sea.

Papyrus was cut and loaded in bundles into a long-
prowed boat. On shore it was baled. An inscription, dated
1475 B.C., depicts the harvesting of the papyrus plant.

The Preparation of Papyrus

The stem of the papyrus plant was slit lengthwise into thin strips 16" long. A layer of the strips was laid ver-
tically side by side. A second layer was placed horizontally,
at right angles over the first layer. The two layers were

pounded and glued together either by a gummy substance or
by water from the River Nile. The uneven edges were
trimmed and the yellow-white sheet of papyrus was rubbed
with pumice to smooth the writing surface.

The sheets of papyrus were then pasted together into
a strip, six inches high and occasionally as much as 100 feet
long. The top and bottom of the strip were reinforced with
papyrus. The strip was then rolled around a rod, usually
made of tightly compressed papyrus.

Since the papyrus was brittle and easily torn, a cover
of papyrus, dyed purple, was often used to protect the roll.
From the end of the roll a tag or ticket was hung, bearing
the title of the roll. The Romans also wrote on papyrus rolls.
They called the rolls volumen, from which comes the word
volume.

The Scribe at Work

The scribe often worked out-of-doors, squatting cross-
legged at a low desk. In a case he carried two reed pens
and water to mix the ink as he copied. Inks were red and
black, the red being used for introducing a new paragraph.
These red letters, or rubrics (from the Latin ruber, meaning red), decorated manuscripts copied in the medieval monasteries and are often used in the printing of modern fine books.
Lampblack was mixed with a gum to produce the black ink.
Oxide of iron formed the basis for red ink. Many representa-
tions of the scribe show him carrying a pen behind each ear,
one for black ink and one for red.

The reed pen, called a calanus, was half-pen and
half-brush. One end of the reed was chewed into a tuft, as
a sharp writing implement would have penetrated the papyrus.

The scribe copied in page-like sections on the roll,
like this:

```
xxxxx   xxxxx   xxxxx   xxxxx   xxxxx
xxxxx   xxxxx   xxxxx   xxxxx   xxxxx
xxxxx   xxxxx   xxxxx   xxxxx   xxxxx
xxxxx   xxxxx   xxxxx   xxxxx   xxxxx
```

The reader unrolled the papyrus with his right hand and
rolled it under with his left hand.

Occasionally, if there was not sufficient room on a papyrus roll to complete the work, the scribe would stop copying in the middle of a word, or cram the ending into a word or two of his own devising.

Papyrus was used as a writing material for a thousand years. The last extant piece, a Papal Bull, was dated 1022 A.D. An amusing letter written on papyrus, after paper was in use, began with the words, "Please pardon the papyrus." Perhaps you've received a letter beginning, "Don't mind this pencil. I can't find my pen."

WOOD AND THE WAX TABLET

Your great grandparents may have copied and recopied their alphabet on a slate, erasing with a damp cloth or with spit and a shirt sleeve in order to practice their "sums." Or your mother may have a slate hanging on the kitchen wall for family messages. The Romans used the idea of a slate as a writing surface when they designed, centuries ago, a wax tablet.

A small block of wood was hollowed and filled with a thin layer of yellow or black wax. The wooden edges of the tablet might be gaily decorated or inlaid with ivory. The writing implement was a pointed stylus of wood or ivory, blunted at one end for erasures. The letters were dug into the wax. When the tablet had served its purpose, the wax was smoothed with the blunt edge of the stylus and the tablet re-used.

A Roman schoolboy wore a wax tablet fastened to his belt, conveniently at hand for the copying of his lessons. Two or three wax tablets were often fastened together by a leather thong, perhaps the first step in the change from a roll to a codex (the basic book form).

Wax tablets were seldom stored in libraries, since the messages scratched on them were usually ephemeral (of no lasting importance). Several wax tablets were found in the ruins of Herculaneum, a city buried in ash and lava when Mt. Vesuvius erupted.

The Romans also used a wooden bulletin board resembling our roadside bill boards. Painted black, the bulletin

boards were set up in the market places. In large, white
letters, the "news," public notes, and even songs were written. The famous laws of Solon were thus displayed for the
Roman citizens.

The next roadside display board you see, be reminded
that it is an old Roman custom adapted to modern use.

PERGAMENA OR PARCHMENT

The Romans must have found wood and papyrus awkward and expensive writing materials. Then a new writing
surface came into use in the city-state of Pergamum in Asia
Minor. This material was parchment--and it can be made
as easily in your classroom as it was in Pergamum.

About 200 B.C. an Egyptian Ptolemy placed an embargo on papyrus, no doubt to raise the price. Furthermore he
was jealous of the great library at Pergamum, which he
feared would out-rival the Alexandrian Library in Egypt unless the supply of papyrus was cut off.

The embargo failed in its purpose. As the story is
told, a scribe in Pergamum made parchment out of sheepskin and called it pergamena in honor of his city. Soon
parchment began to replace papyrus as a writing material.

A Sheet of Parchment

Buy a sheepskin from a butcher. Soak the skin in lye
for several hours. Scrape off the wool and fatty substance
with a sharp knife. While the skin is wet, stretch it and
nail it onto a wooden frame or to the floor. When the skin
is dry, use pumice or an abrasive to clean the skin. Rub
in chalk dust to whiten it. Trim and cut it into small sheets.
Then you will understand that it took the skins of 300 sheep
to make a medieval manuscript.

In writing on parchment a quill pen of goose or turkey
feathers was used. It was dipped into a brownish ink made
from gall nuts that grow on the bark of the oak tree.

If you wish to make vellum instead of parchment, follow the same procedure using calfskin instead of sheepskin.

Vellum is a delicate, smooth and white writing surface that
takes ink perfectly.

The Papyrus and Parchment Codex

The parchment was, at first, rolled like the papyrus,
with the writing in page-like sections on the roll. However,
by the first century A. D. the Romans began to experiment
with a new form of the roll. The parchment was folded once
and the writing was done on the skin side. Then the parchment was folded back and forth in an accordion pleated fashion.

The folded parchment pages were stiff and bulky and
awkward to handle. Heavy, wooden covers were placed at
the front and at the back. Holes were punched through the
covers and the parchment pages. Leather thongs were run
through the holes. In spite of the wooden covers, the parchment "book" did not close. Metal clasps were nailed to the
covers and, to give further weight to the covers, metal corners called bosses were added. The codex--from the Latin
word caudex, meaning wood--became the essential form of
the book you are holding as you read this chapter.

The spine or back of the codex was unsightly. Leather was stretched over the spine and wooden covers. The
ragged edges of the leather were nailed to the inside covers
of the large codex. It is not surprising that one day a scribe
or a binder seized a piece of used parchment and pasted it
over the inside cover as an end paper. Often these parchment end papers are of more interest to scholars than the
contents of the codex, as scraps of old music or an ancient
literary work have been discovered on end papers.

The Romans illustrated their rolls and codices with
portraits. Varro used 700 portraits in his ancient Roman
"Who's Who. " Aristotle's writings, especially those on Anat-
omy, had many explanatory drawings.

Until the printed book, the parchment codex remained
the basic form of the book. In medieval times, the monastic
scribes and the artists beautified the text of the manuscript
with hand writing and illumination. The covers of the codex
were decorated with designs cut into the leather, with inlays
of ivory, chunks of quartz and great metal crosses. But the
crowning glory were the jeweled bindings. Gold filigree was

laid over the leather and encrusted with diamonds, pearls
and rubies--a gift to enhance a church altar, the library of
a King or the book chest of a Lady at Court. One of these
magnificent jeweled bindings is on display at the Pierpont
Morgan Library in New York City.

The story of parchment as a writing material is in-
complete without mentioning hidden writing. Imagine a monastic scribe searching for an extra piece of parchment to complete the copying of a religious work. Upon finding a piece
of used parchment, he erased the writing on it and completed
his copying. Then imagine a scholar, years later who read
the manuscript (St. Augustine's discussion of the Psalms)
and discovered a faint trace of early writing. Underneath
the erasure was a priceless page of manuscript--Cicero's
De Republica, now treasured by the Vatican Library. This
twice-used parchment is known as a palimpsest.

As the second century closed and as the Romans were
experimenting with papyrus and parchment codices, a Chinese
invented a new writing material--paper.

PAPER: A UNIVERSAL WRITING MATERIAL

Over a thousand years before Johann Gutenberg carefully selected the paper for his first printed book, a Chinese,
T'sai Lun, had mixed bark, hemp, fish nets and rags with
water. He had invented paper. This secret process was re-
ported to his Emperor and T'sai Lun was rewarded. A temple was built in his honor and Chinese sellers of paper
burned incense before his picture.

By the 5th century A.D., paper rather than silk or
bamboo was used almost exclusively as the material upon
which the Chinese wrote.

The Tun-Huang Papers

In 1907, Sir Aurel Stein, on one of his many archeological expeditions, arrived at the Cave of the Thousand
Buddhas near the Great Wall of China. Here he learned that
a priest had discovered in a cave a secret chamber piled
high with documents. Some were written on silk and bamboo,
but nine letters were written on rag paper. They are dated

about 50 years after T'sai Lun first made paper. One of
these letters is preserved in the British Museum, London.

Sir Aurel named the "find" the Tun-Huang Papers in
honor of the nearby village of Tun-Huang. They are the
earliest known examples of paper in existence.

The Secret of Paper Making Revealed

What were the events that forced the diffusion of this
secret invention beyond the Chinese borders? Commerce,
war and religion supply the answer.

Traders loaded their camel caravans with spices, tea,
jewels, cloth and paper, and began the slow trek westward.

The Moslems in the 8th century A.D., boasting that
they would conquer the world, advanced toward the East.
Among the prisoners taken were Chinese paper makers, who
were forced to reveal their secret and make paper for their
conquerors. The Moslems jealously guarded paper for their
exclusive use and promptly closed the trade routes to Europe,
thus withholding for centuries the use of paper by the Europeans.

In spite of these delays, by 700 A.D. paper was made
in the ancient city of Samarkand (now in the U.S.S.R.). This
was the first paper to be made outside of China, but paper
had made a small step on its journey to Europe.

The Westward Journey of Paper

If you can secure at the school bookstore a map of
the world it might be interesting to chart with a red pencil
the westward journey of paper. Start with Tun-Huang, a pin-
point dot on the map of China, and move the red pencil to
Samarkand.

For centuries paper making flourished in Samarkand
and paper became a profitable commercial product. Chinese
prisoners, who were forced to make paper in Samarkand,
found available the finest of flax and hemp for making high
quality paper.

Now draw a red line from Samarkand to the exotic

city of Baghdad. Harun-al-Rashid, who bade Scheherazade
tell him a new Arabian Night's tale for 1001 nights, brought
Chinese paper makers and their art to this royal city.

Extraordinarily fine paper was made in Damascus.
This was fortunate for Europe, as Damascus paper was loaded onto camel caravans bound for Italy.

If your red line is at Damascus, it will now be neces-
sary to draw two diverging lines on your map, one from
Damascus to southern Italy and another from Damascus to
Cairo, Egypt.

The Moslems, who had guarded the secret of paper
making for 500 years, now advanced across North Africa on
the way to conquer Spain and then all of Europe. In Egypt
they taught the Egyptians the art of making paper. Abundant
flax and linen cloth made possible an excellent grade of paper. Thousands of paper documents concerning Moslem culture were preserved in this rainless country.

With your red pencil follow the conquering Moslems
across Egypt to Fez, Morocco and on to Spain.

Under Moslem rule, the first paper mill in Europe
was built at Jativa, Spain in 1150 A.D. Have you found
Jativa on the map?

The use of paper grew at an impressive rate and the
making of paper spilled over into France.

Meanwhile follow the red line from Damascus to Fabriano, Italy. Here, in 1270 A.D. appeared the first paper mill
in Christendom--the famous Fabriano mills. The finest hand
made paper was produced here.

The Italian artisans carried the paper making process
across the Alps to Nuremberg, Germany.

Has your red pencil arrived at Nuremberg? If so,
pause a moment to pay tribute to a very notable paper mill--
the Stomer Mills--before you draw the red line across Germany to Cologne and, at last, across to England.

The Europeans were slow to adopt paper as a writing
material. They considered parchment more satisfactory.
Educational advancement was slow and the demand for books

small.   The church frowned on papyrus as it was Moslem in
origin.   Not until the arrival of the printed book did paper
come into universal use.

The first mill in the New World was built at Philadelphia in the late 1600s.   Carry the red line across the At-
lantic ocean to Philadelphia and on to your home town.   Relics
of an old paper mill or a street named Paper Mill Road are
to be found in many small towns in the United States.

Handmade Paper

The craft of making rag paper by hand has changed
little since its invention by T'sai Lun in 105 A.D.

The Process.   Shred linen rags and mix them with
warm water.   Pour these fibers into a vat.   Stir constantly
with a paddle.   Prepare a mold or frame.   Plunge the mold
perpendicularly into the vat of emasculated fibers, then turn
the mold to a horizontal position.   Lift the mold and let the
water drain off.   Shake the pulp on the mold back and forth
until the fibers cross and mat.   Dry the pulp on the mold in
the sun as the Chinese did, or flip the pulpy paper onto a
piece of felt, cover it with another felt and apply pressure
until the sheet is dry.   The paper will be rough, but should
not be thick and thin in spots.   To finish the paper so that
it will carry ink, size it by dipping it in animal glue or
starch.   Dry it again between felts.   You have made paper.

The Mold or Frame.   What is a mold?   A piece of
fine wire screen, bordered with a stout frame, with another
removable frame within the mold.

This second frame is known as a deckle and deter-
mines the size of the sheet of paper.   When the fibers are
matted, the inner frame or deckle is removed leaving an uneven, frayed edge on the paper--a deckle edge.   Often an
imitation of this edge will appear on machine-made paper.

To fill a mold with wet pulp might well tear the fine
wire mesh off the frame.   Hence, heavier wires are placed
one inch apart at right angles to the fine wires.   These heavy
wires leave imprints in the paper called chain lines.   Hold
this sheet of paper up to the light.   Can you see the chain
lines?   If you can, then the paper is laid paper.   When there
are no chain lines and the paper resembles vellum, it is know
as wove paper.

Many beautiful and expensive books today are hand-
printed on handmade paper and may be considered an art
comparable to hand weaving or painting.

Machine-Made Paper

In the beginning, machine-made paper paralleled the
process of making paper by hand.   Some use was made of
such machines as the screw press.   The laborers were given
special jobs with appropriate titles such as vatman and coucher.   Paper could now be produced in quantity.

When paper was made in the early mills--the Fabriano Mills in Italy and the Stomer Mills in Germany--the
fibers were usually linen rags.   Placed in a huge vat of
warm water, the fibers were stirred constantly by the vatman.   The coucher handled the mold and tipped the pulp onto
the felts.   When a pile of paper and felts was high, it was
placed in a screw press and the water squeezed out.   Then,
without the felts, the paper was pressed three times.

Three or four sheets of paper, called spurs, were
hung to dry over horsehair cords in a loft.   Sizing of glue
or starch was applied and the paper was pressed.   Sizing to
prevent the blotting of inks on machine-made paper was first
used in the Fabriano Mills.

The Watermark.   Seven hundred years ago a watermark was designed and used in the paper making process at
the Fabriano Mills.

A watermark in paper results from a design made of
very fine wire, laid on top of the mold.   As pressure is
placed on the damp paper, the imprint of the watermark is
transferred to the paper.

Again, hold to the light the page you are reading.   Is
there a watermark in the paper?   It may be the name or the
trade mark of the printer; the head of a fool with cap and
bells; a bunch of grapes or a flower.   Not all paper is water-
marked but keep looking in books or at the paper you use in
typing class until you find a watermark.

Watermarks serve several purposes:

In early printed books with no date or printer's name,

the watermark often identified the size and number of
pages in the book as well as the name of the printer,
providing he used paper with a particular watermark.

To be certain that a rare and valuable book is neither
a fake nor a counterfeit, both the paper and the watermark can be used to verify the authenticity. The Thomas J. Wise forgeries serve as an example. Mr. Wise,
a collector of rare books and a reputable scholar,
claimed he had "discovered" the only known copies of
pamphlets of 19th century English verse. The paper on
which the pamphlets were printed had been made many
years after the pamphlets were published. Paper revealed the hoax.

Commercial printing plants often use a watermark for
advertising purposes or as a matter of pride. For example, the watermark of a fine printing house is "John-
stone Bond. "

Watermarks may also indicate the quality of the paper,
e. g. , Bond.

William Morris, a designer and printer of fine books,
believed that the watermark contributed to the beauty of
handmade paper. He named the paper he created The
Flower, The Perch, The Apple after the watermarks of
flower, fish and fruit.

There are many people whose interest in watermarks
becomes a hobby. Are you aware of the diversity of watermarks? When you pick up a sheet of paper, do you look for
the watermark? The old cliché, "the eye sees only what it
knows," operates in many areas.

The Modern Paper Mill. The paper making industry
is moving so rapidly that facts written about it today will be
out-of-date tomorrow. Mechanization of all processes is the
major factor in the industry's development.

A field trip to a paper mill is the most satisfactory
way of getting up-to-date factual and visual information about
the process. Perhaps your teacher will help you arrange a
trip to a mill.

However, a few facts about modern machine made paper will make you an intelligent visitor.

1. Review the process of making paper by hand, remembering such terms as: fibers, vatman, coucher, mold, deckle, felts, chain lines and watermarks. This review will help you to recognize the processes of machine-made paper, which basically are the same as those employed in making handmade paper.

2. Paper making by hand or by machine begins with the fibers--rags, wood pulp, bamboo, cereal straw, Esparto grass, plastics, synthetics, recycled paper or waste paper. The recovering of paper is a difficult process; the source of the waste paper, how it is gathered, and the best way to restore the original fibers must all be considered. Additives such as asphalt, metal foil and plastics are used to strengthen the waste paper fibers. A decision must also be made as to whether to de-ink or not, that is, to remove printed matter on the waste paper.

When you visit a paper mill, ask carefully about the fibers used to make the stock. Don't be surprised if popcorn is being used.

3. Instead of hand-dipping the mold into the stock, draining the water and meshing the fibers by moving the mold back and forth, a huge machine, 100 feet long, does the work.

This machine is the Fourdrinier, named in honor of the Fourdrinier brothers who invented the machine. Some authorities claim, however, that Louis Robert made the first machine for a famous French printing house.

The Fourdrinier appears almost human as it receives the stock from the Hollander (beater) and on a wide screen belt moves the stock back and forth as well as lengthwise. As the water drains, the stock is contained by powerful jets of water.

If a watermark is to be used a lightweight wire roll called a dandy roll is fastened to the bed of the Fourdrinier. The dandy roll bears the design of the watermark and, as in handmade paper, leaves a thin spot on the paper, making the design visible because of greater transmission of light.

As the stock nears the end of the Fourdrinier, a small, very heavy roll, the couch roll, presses the paper dry and the finishing process begins.

Finishing is the operation that makes paper useful. Great, whirling hot and cold rolls receive the paper from the machine and prepare different grades depending on the manner of conversion. In wet conversion, paper is impregnated or laminated, usually with petrochemicals, resulting in a smooth writing surface. Dry conversion is used in the production of lower grades of paper.

Paper is usually graded in five categories: Bond, a stiff, durable paper; Book paper; Bristol; Newsprint and Kraft, used for wrapping paper and paper bags.

A visit to a paper mill will give you an opportunity to check what you have read on the preceding pages about paper making.

The typewriter and the computer as writing instruments are a far cry from a flint, a pointed stick or a goose quill. Photographic papers, magnetic tape and film, as writing materials of the future, prove again the statement, "The materials upon which man writes determine to a large extent his manner of writing."

WRITING MATERIALS: A REVIEW

From a piece of bone to a Xerox copying machine, the materials upon which man writes have influenced the manner of his writing.

The wedge-shaped cuneiform characters on clay; hieroglyphics drawn on papyrus; high-shouldered, black letter Gothic on parchment; a "Gutenberg" on paper; the write-outs of computers on plastic paper, and the billions of feet of film and tape indicate that writing materials change as man endeavors to record and to communicate his ideas with greater ease and speed.

Paper has been the major material upon which man's written records have been transmitted. The amount of paper used today in the United States is mind-boggling.

Commercially, paper is one of our major products and paper companies boast that they "paper the world." However, the source materials for making paper, like many other endangered products, are becoming scarce and expensive. Other materials will replace them in the everlasting cycle of change and growth.

Your children's children may well begin a letter--if letters are written then--with the words, "Please pardon the paper."

EXTRA CREDIT PROJECTS

Discuss these projects with your teacher, especially your art teacher. The sources of required materials and the uses of the completed projects should be considered. Group work may be the best way to handle the projects although they can be successfully carried out by individuals.

1. Using the "recipes" given in the chapter, make a sheet of papyrus, parchment and paper. Write on them a word or two in symbols appropriate to the material: e.g., hieroglyphs on the papyrus, uncials on the parchment.

2. Use river or manufactured clay and make a clay tablet. Draw cuneiform symbols on it.

3. Make a wax tablet and, with a stylus, write on it several square capitals of the alphabet as the Roman schoolboy did.

4. Construct a codex with an untanned leather cover, clasps and bosses.

These completed projects, if shown with a beautiful modern book, will provide a story of the development of the form of the book. Why not use the projects for a display in the library?

You will find that a book by Ogg, titled The 26 Letters, will be of help in the projects.

Plan a visit to a paper mill. Prepare your class mates for the visit by displaying pictures and samples of various types of paper. Make use of the map you drew on the westward journey of paper. Films on paper making are

numerous. Paper mills will send you most interesting free
and inexpensive material.

FURTHER READING

Chiera, Edward. They Wrote on Clay. Chicago: University
    of Chicago Press, 1938.
        A straightforward account of the exploration and pos-
sible solution of archeological puzzles unearthed in ancient
Babylonia. Emphasis on books and libraries. Many pictures.
A book to read and re-read if you are considering archeology as a career.

Hunter, Dard. Paper Making, the History and Technique of
    an Ancient Craft. 2d ed., rev. and enl. New York:
    Knopf, 1947.
        A master of the craft and its history may tell you
more than you care to know about paper making, but he tells
it very well, indeed. His autobiography, My Life with Paper,
is delightful reading.

McMurtrie, Douglas. The Book: The Story of Printing and
    Book Making. New York: Oxford University Press, ©
    1943.
        The "official textbook" on the history of the book.
The first 75 pages are pertinent to writing materials.

Vervliet, Hendrik D. L., ed. The Book through 5,000
    Years. Phaedon, 1972.
        This book, covering from "clay to our day," was
written by a team of scholars. A large and expensive book
(it weighs eight pounds). The title is included on this list
to make you aware not only of the vast extent of material it
is possible to gather on the history of the book, but that
learned men devote time and effort to a study of the subject.

Chapter 3

"THE HOUSE OF THE TABLET"

"What's past is prologue"
--Shakespeare

It may appear odd to begin the story of ancient libraries with a suggestion of a possible career for you.

Archeology is more than digging holes in the ground.
It demands a high quality of scholarship, a knowledge of ancient languages, a carefully controlled imagination and endless patience. Every tiny piece of unearthed stone or bone
may tell a story.

Perhaps one day you will look down into a 4,000 year-
old tomb excavated from a tell (mound) crowded with chariots,
household furniture, clay tablets, gold helmets, the bodies of
oxen, soldiers and women surrounding the body of a King.

Why not consider archeology as a profession? You
might find yourself re-writing history.

What have archeologists told us about ancient libraries?

THE LIBRARIES OF THE SUMERIANS,
BABYLONIANS, ASSYRIANS

In the fertile valleys of Asia Minor, washed by the
Tigris and Euphrates rivers, lay the land of the Sumerians,
the cradle of civilization. In time, the Sumerians were conquered by the Babylonians who, in turn, were forced in 1100
B.C. to surrender their country and their culture to the As-

37

syrians.   Instead of total destruction of the conquered, the
conquerors wisely built upon their strengths.

The Sumerians, Babylonians and Assyrians centered
their culture about a capital city--Ur, Babylon and Ninevah
respectively.   Archeologists have excavated seven layers of
Ur, each built on the site of the others, the lowest level being
dated 5000 B. C.   Babylon and Ninevah have also been partly
restored.

In the jigsaw patterns of these cities, built and rebuilt of clay bricks baked in the sun, have been found temples, palaces, market places and tons of clay tablets bearing records of this early civilization.   In the temples built
for the worship of the gods was focused the life of the city:
schools for scribes, industry, government and records.   A
payroll listed the names of women receiving money for weaving cloth.   Merchants loaned money at 20% interest.   Tax
memoranda numbered 100,000.   These temple records on
clay were the first libraries of Mesopotamia.

However, the Stele of Hammurabi, the Library of Assurbanipal and the Tell-el-Amarna Tablets are facts of history, and upon them clearly rests the story of ancient libraries.

The Stele of Hammurabi

A stele was a monument-like slab of hard baked clay
with writing on the front and back.   Set up in market places
of cities in the land, a stele was an ancient newspaper.   The
triumphs of war, edicts of kings, disasters and hymns to the
gods were written on stelae for the people to read.   The early Egyptians used stelae for the same purposes.   However,
Egyptian stelae were pointed four-sided monuments called
obelisks.   A famous example of an Egyptian obelisk is Cleopatra's Needle in Central Park, New York City.

Several codes of laws have been unearthed, the best
known being the Code of Hammurabi, a wise and powerful
Babylonian king.   History has long honored the Romans for
a codification of the laws, but Hammurabi, two thousand years
before the Romans, established the laws of his land and ordered that these laws be written on stelae and set in the
market places of his kingdom.

An archeologist, digging in Susa, Persia (now Iran), found one of Hammurabi's stelae. Into the top of the short pillar was cut a picture of Hammurabi receiving the laws from a god. Then followed the laws, written in cuneiform.

What does all this have to do with libraries? If you believe that the major purposes of a library are to store and to spread knowledge, then the stelae were libraries.

Babylonian libraries were also archives in which were accumulated on clay tablets the records of the kingdom. As the Babylonians added literary, scientific and religious tablets to the collection, an authentic library emerged. In fact, in the records of a Babylonian temple library, a librarian, Amit Anu was honored. With full assurance, it can be stated that the Babylonians had libraries, arranged and supervised by librarians.

Considerable information, however, is available about Assyrian libraries in the temples and in the palaces of kings --Sargon, Sennacherib and Assurbanipal.

The Library of Assurbanipal at Ninevah

In Ninevah, the capital city of the Assyrians, Assurbanipal, 668-626 B.C., gathered in his palace library all the knowledge he could find in this ancient world. Assurbanipal, unlike other early kings, claimed he could read and write. At least, he held learning in high regard.

Archeologists have uncovered documents (clay tablets) that reveal Assurbanipal's method for gathering this knowledge. A letter sent by Assurbanipal to his subjects demonstrates the nature of his book collecting activities:

> Word of the king to Shaduni. It is well with me; mayest thou be happy ... take with thee three men ... seek out all the tablets, all those that are in their houses and all that are deposited in the temple ... that may be profitable for my place, seek them out, pick them up and send to me. *

---

*Edward Chiera. They Wrote on Clay (Chicago: University of Chicago Press, c. 1938), p. 174.

Using this royal power, Assurbanipal gathered 25,000
clay tablets into the many rooms of his palace library.
There was a room for history and the famous King's list and
there were others for treaties; for geography describing
towns, countries, rivers and mountains; for laws; for tax
lists, and finally for myths and legends.

The palace was dug out over a hundred years ago by
an English archeologist, Sir Henry Rawlinson, from a tell
(mound) known as the Lamb.   The palace and its library had
lain hidden for 25 centuries.   The Chaldeans invaded Ninevah
in 612 B. C., and having little regard for the clay tablets,
they used a battering ram to push the walls of the library
together, burying the tablets in rubble and hence preserving
them.   Counting whole tablets and fragments, 21,000 tablets
are now in the British Museum, London.

Where was this famous library?   In the palace of
Assurbanipal at Ninevah.   Whether it was open to the public
is not known.

The Care and Arrangement of the Tablets.   The records were written on thousands of clay tablets.   It must be
noted that more than one tablet was required to carry a legend or a law.   The tablets were numbered in series; for example, "the 15th tablet of the evil spirits." Catchwords
were used to keep the clay tablets in logical progression--
just as they are today to indicate the order of pages of a
book.   The last word on a tablet was repeated as the first
word on a succeeding tablet.   Discovered in the ruins were
catalogs or lists of the tablets, entered by title and first line.
Evidently an attempt had been made to organize the library.

The tablets comprising a "book" were kept in clay
jars, bins, baskets or pigeon-hole shelving.

Each tablet in Assurbanipal's library was stamped
with a mark of ownership--"Assurbanipal, King of the World."
When you next place your book plate in a new book for your
shelves, be reminded that Assurbanipal had his book plate
chiseled on his clay tablets 600 years before Christ was
born.

As in monastic libraries centuries later, a curse
was placed on him who stole a tablet from the Royal library.

The Tablet Keepers.   Records dated centuries before

the reign of Assurbanipal were unearthed at Ur. A tablet
bore the name of a librarian, Amit Anu, Keeper of the Tablets. Deciphered from a tablet in Assurbanipal's library was
also the name Nabu-Zuqub-ging (The Man of the Written Tablet). A librarian served a long apprenticeship; not only did
he have to learn how to write the complicated cuneiform characters, but he had to be proficient in many languages.

The Contents of the Royal Library. Scholars can tell
us a great deal about the contents since the discovery of a
key to cuneiform writing made it possible to decipher the
clay tablets.

Tablets were copied in great numbers. Translations
from the Babylonian to the Assyrian language were written
in the spaces between the lines of characters on the tablets.
Foreign language dictionaries were compiled, comparable to
a Spanish-English dictionary of today.

Thousands of contracts were recorded on clay and by
an almost magic process enclosed in clay envelopes. The
Mesopotamians were insistent on a written contract, whether
for the purchase of an ox or a few cereal grains. Scribes
gathered in the market place or sat at the city gate. The
signing of both parties of the contract was often done by fingerprinting. Did you think fingerprinting began with Scotland
Yard?

Contracts were also signed with seals. Each citizen
wore on a leather thong around his neck a small clay seal or
stamp of identification. The seal, engraved with religious
symbols or with the mark of a profession such as the instruments of a surgeon, was a citizen's signature. The seal was
pressed into the wet clay on which the contract was written,
and thus the bargain was "sealed."

Quantities of clay tablets contained material on medicine and science, overshadowed by magic, omens and in-
cantations. It was believed that diseases were caused by
demons. Epidemics were much feared and to stop the transmission of a disease, a goat was laid by the body of the sick
person in the hope that the disease would pass to the goat
rather than to another member of the family. Ageless reme-
dies were used: hot oil for earaches and a mixture of beer
and olive oil for growing hair on a bald head. The cost of
major and minor surgery was clearly stated in the laws. If
an important man died as the result of an operation, the surgeon lost his right hand.

Much was known of astronomy and astrology. Time
was told and a calendar arranged by the movement of the
stars. Geographical facts were limited; it was believed that
the earth was flat and map-makers indulged their imaginations.

Archeologists have found quantities of copybooks used
in teaching writing to a school of scribes. Samples of a
teacher's writing and the first miserable attempts of the
scribes are reminiscent of the way you were taught to write.
Only you threw the scrap paper in the basket. The clay tablets were preserved in the library room. Unearthed in a
bas-relief (engravings on clay) is a depiction of a secretary-
scribe taking dictation.

The literature was full of colorful and fascinating legends, the most famous being the story of the Creation.
Shrouded in mystery, the Gilgamesh, of which only fragments
have been found, sets forth the story as follows:

> In the beginning was only water. Came the gods,
> Timat, the mother of Chaos, being the most power-
> ful. All the other gods sought to destroy her, and,
> at last, the west wind blew in her mouth, splitting
> her in two. One half of her became the earth, the
> other half the heavens.

Another legend grew and was recorded about a great
flood unleashed by the gods. A few people were saved by
the goddess of love. This legend parallels the Biblical account of Noah's Ark.

Libraries of clay tablets have also been uncovered at
Kish, Sippar and Nippur, attesting to the fact that the Babylonians and Assyrians enjoyed an amazing civilization which
was far from primitive. We would know little about Mesopotamian history without libraries.

The Tell-el-Amarna Tablets

Not too many years ago, an Arab woman found some
clay in Egypt. They are now known as the Tell-el-Amarna
tablets in honor of the village in which they were discovered.

How very strange to find clay tablets appearing in a
kingdom whose people wrote in hieroglyphics and used papyrus as a writing material. Before scholars realized the im-

portance of the find, the tablets were broken up and sold to museums in Europe and America.

The tablets, written in cuneiform and dated 1500 B. C., are a record of diplomatic correspondence between the King of Babylonia and a pharaoh of Egypt. The Egyptians were accused of being stingy with gold from the mines on Sinai. The Babylonians, greatly desirous of staying on the gold standard, threatened the Egyptians, claiming that in Egypt gold was as plentiful as the dust of the earth.

Certain fragments of the Tell-el-Amarna tablets indicate that an Egyptian scribe pondered over the strange cuneiform writing as he marked in red ink what he considered to be the end of one word and the beginning of the next.

Some day, someone may find letters of the pharaoh, responding to the Babylonian king and denying his request, thus provoking an "incident"--a preview of early international politics.

The clay tablet has told the story of Mesopotamian libraries. The story of Egyptian libraries cannot be so easily told because of the nature of the material upon which they wrote.

THE LIBRARIES OF THE EGYPTIANS

Archeologists have dug in Egypt. Scholars have carefully studied the ruins. Egyptologists have effected restorations. Nevertheless, our knowledge of Egyptian libraries is much less than our knowledge of Assyrian libraries. Why? The Egyptians wrote on fragile papyrus. The Assyrians wrote on clay. Only a few shreds of papyrus have been found. Clay tablets shout out ancient Mesopotamian culture.

The Culture of Early Egypt

What is known of Egyptian culture has been determined from the magnificent trappings of excavated tombs and temples, from wall inscriptions and from Greek scholars who recounted Egyptian history.

The Egyptians worshipped many gods and built temples

to their glory.   Here lived the well-educated priests who
served the gods.   Here, too, were the law courts, granaries,
workshops, schools and libraries.

The Egyptians venerated writing and learning.   One
reads of the great joy of a father taking his son up the Nile
to school in 1300 B.C.   Scribes were held in high regard.
As boy apprentices, they were obliged to serve many years
before attaining the title of scribe.   They had to learn to
write 700 hieroglyphic characters, and often the characters
had two or three meanings.   Libraries containing text books
and grammars were an important part of the training schools
for scribes.

A rich culture flourished in early Egypt.   A calendar
was devised, the year divided into 12 months of 30 days with
night and day each 12 hours long.   The calendar was based
on the rising of the dog star, Sirius.

Mathematics was a highly developed science.   In common use were fractions and a decimal system based on the
number 10.   Medical lore was so involved with magic that it
was difficult to define the bounds of either.   Magic and super-
stition are as old as man.   Unlucky days were carefully observed, and even in today's culture, Friday the 13th is regarded as a poor day to begin a journey.

Myths, tales of Creation, short stories, poetry, love
songs and hymns comprising their literary lore were dedicated to the gods.

The Egyptians farmed, traded and manufactured goods.
Such items as glass, pottery, linen cloth were exported.
Fish, wine and ivory were imported from other countries.
Their libraries held the records of this flourishing civiliza-
tion.   But scholars estimate that less than one per cent of
what was written on papyrus has come down to us.

An Overview of Egyptian Libraries

In excavating a temple at Thebes, archeologists found
a room bearing over its portal the hieroglyphics--"Dispensary
of the Soul. "   Since the papyrus rolls it undoubtedly contained
had either disintegrated or been stolen, no one knows what
was in that library room.

Near an excavated temple were found the tombs of
two librarians, a father and son. A tomb inscription bore
the name of a librarian, Amen-em-haut, and records revealed
that in the temple of Thoth a woman served as an assistant
librarian. Such titles as Keeper of the Scrolls, Scribe and
Priest, Scribe of the Secret Writing, and Scribe of the King's
Archives were bestowed upon librarians.

Champollion, the Frenchman who deciphered the Rosetta Stone, uncovered at Karnak a temple under the protection
of the god, Thoth.   The library room bore the inscription,
"House of Books. " But no papyrus rolls!

Several libraries in the homes of wealthy Egyptians
have been excavated. Rolls were stored in jars and in
jeweled cases. In the rubble, a roll was found on which had
been written an extensive grocery list covering two weeks'
supplies for a large family.

The early libraries of Egypt were housed in the temples and supervised by a librarian. Vast stores of papyrus
rolls recorded life and times in Egypt.

The Library at Edfu

A most unusual school room and a library were uncovered in the temple at Edfu. On the walls of the library
were carved sacred texts, drawings of writing instruments
used by the scribes and a catalog of the papyrus rolls--not
a card catalog but a wall catalog, listing, among other subjects, a great quantity of rolls on Magic.

Scholars who can decipher hieroglyphic writing have
found 21 different subjects under which the rolls were classified. For example, this hieroglyph ⟨symbols⟩ indicated
rolls on Horoscopes. How strange if you went into a modern library to search for books on Transportation and found
on the library wall this symbol ⟨symbols⟩ ! But what would an
Egyptian student think of a computer feeding back a dozen
titles on Transportation at the touch of a button?

It is not known how many rolls were stored at Edfu.
None was found in the library room when the temple was
opened. If only the Egyptians has used a more sturdy writing material than papyrus!

The Book of the Dead

Tombs have disclosed interesting "individual" libraries
known as the Book of the Dead. Fragments of one of these
rolls, dated 1800 B.C., are preserved in the British Museum,
London.

The Egyptians usually buried their dead surrounded by
lavish possessions for an existence in the next world. Included in these trappings was a Book of the Dead in which was
recorded the life of the deceased and instructions as to how
he should travel in the next world. The text varied in length
according to the wealth and importance of the dead.

If these Books of the Dead had been assembled in the
library room of a temple, the collection might well be compared to a biography section in a modern library.

The grandeur of Egyptian culture was destroyed by the
conquests of the Assyrians and Persians. Scholars and
priests were killed, temple libraries were ravished. A brief
revival of learning under the Ptolemies was influenced largely
by Greek culture.

THE LITERARY HERITAGE OF GREECE

Although centuries have passed, the stories of Odysseus and Circe, of Odysseus and the one-eyed giant, Poly-
phemus, and of Jason and the Golden Fleece still hold charm
and excitement for a world besieged by the noisy outpourings
of communication media. The old tales are said to have been
recited 900 years before Christ by the legendary Homer as
he wandered the countryside.

The early Greeks used the spoken word to enrich their
culture--tragic dramas and delightful comedies played in amphi-
theatres and stormy dialogues in their law courts. Scholars
and pupils walked the groves, declaiming theories of life and
death. Love poems and stories of the glorious conquests of
Greek heroes were sung by the bards.

THE GOLDEN AGE OF GREEK LIBRARIES

Although the evidence is thin, it can be assumed that

by 600 B.C. a reading public had developed in Greece.
Schools flourished. Rolls were cheap and sold in large quantity. Pisistratus, a lover of art and music, the philosopher
Plato and the dramatist Euripides gathered large collections
of papyrus rolls and made them available to friends. A library was opened in Athens to provide the public with fair
copies of the popular dramas of Aeschylus, Sophocles and
Euripides.

Aristotle and His Library

With Aristotle (384-322 B.C.) the Greek world moved
from the oral tradition to the art of reading. A pupil of
Plato, the teacher of Alexander the Great, a philosopher, a
scientist and perhaps the greatest thinker the world has known,
Aristotle spread his influence on Greek culture. Many of his
teachings in natural science, logic, politics and psychology
have stood the test of years.

Aristotle's library was extensive and no doubt was consulted freely by Greek scholars. No listing of the titles of
the papyrus rolls has been found. The contents must remain
a mystery except for occasional comments by Greek writers
who consulted books in Aristotle's library.

At his death the library was given to one of his friends.
Lest it be taken to Rome among the spoils of war, the library
was secretly buried. Despite this precaution, in 88 B.C. the
Roman Sulla did carry off what he could find of the badly
damaged papyrus rolls.

Aristotle's books may have been lost to the world, but
his influence has not. At no time in history have libraries
been more honored than in ancient Greece. The glory lived
on in the most magnificent of ancient libraries--the Alexandrian Library.

The Alexandrian Library

In Egypt, on a thumb of land jutting out into the Mediterranean Sea, stood one of the Seven Wonders of the World,
the Lighthouse of Pharos. Not far from this landmark, Alexander the Great, fresh from his mighty conquests, built in
300 B.C. a wondrous city named in his honor, Alexandria.

A brilliant and devoted pupil of Aristotle, Alexander

resolved to make his city a center of world culture by bringing to it Greek scholars; the whole of Greek literature; and
schools, lyceums and theatres to rival those in Athens.

Building the Collection. Alexander's greatest wish,
however, was to build a library similar in plan to Aristotle's
--with covered walks, lecture halls, study rooms, dining
halls, cloisters, gardens filled with statuary, an observatory
and a library. It would be a mecca for thousands of scholars from all over the world.

Accordingly, under Ptolemy I of Egypt and the exiled
scholar, Demetrius of Phalerum, the work began. Scholars
and scribes were gathered into the temples and the collecting,
editing and copying of thousands of papyrus rolls went forward. Although Demetrius was later banished from Egypt for
treason, the library grew into an enormous collection. It
was claimed that the library housed a million rolls--the largest library in the world before the invention of printing. A
more likely estimate is 700,000 rolls, which would probably
equal 100,000 modern books.

Ptolemy I was an avid collector of manuscripts, by
fair means or foul. Using his royal prerogative, he caused
all ships at sea and in the harbors to be seized and searched
for manuscripts. Copies were made, the original manuscripts
kept for the library, and the copies returned. State copies of
the Greek dramas were borrowed and copied, and the State
copies retained. Ptolemy sent scribes to the East to copy
manuscripts in Persia, Islam and far-away India.

The scribes copied the classics with reed pens onto
papyrus rolls. They were paid according to the number of
lines copied. No capital letters were used in the hieratic
script, and no space was left between words. A special sign
denoted the beginning of each paragraph. The writing, instead of extending in a line across the length of the roll, was
done in page-like segments. Imagine how awkward it would
have been to read a line across the top of a roll of papyrus
25 feet long, unrolling and re-rolling in order to begin line
two. Even the stick, resembling a thin rolling pin, around
which the papyrus was wrapped, added little to the convenience of the reader.

Organizing the Library. The Alexandrian library
actually consisted of two libraries--Brucheion and Serapeum--
beautiful buildings, rich in statuary, with tall marble columns,

and alive with teachers and students, reading, discussing and
searching for answers.

Within the library, the papyrus rolls were kept in
pigeon-hole boxes fastened to the wall, the rolls of one book
placed together in a box.   Purple tags hung from the ends
of the rolls, identifying each roll by title and first lines.
The rolls were six to 12 inches tall and 20 to 25 feet long.
Valuable rolls often carried for protection an extra blank
sheet of papyrus--perhaps the first idea of a book cover.
Capsae, resembling hat boxes, made of leather and decorated
with gold, were used for storage or carrying cases.

The Alexandrian Library was arranged under five major subjects or classes: Poetry, History, Philosophy, Ora-
tory and Miscellany.   This was the same classification scheme
as Aristotle used in his private library.   However, as the
collection at Alexandria grew, the original five main divisions
were extended to 120.

The rolls were fully cataloged according to the title,
number of lines, first words and, if possible, the name of
the author.

Distinguished Greek scholars served as librarians at
the Alexandrian: Zenodotus; Eratosthenes, who first measured the circumference of the earth; Aristarchus, a very
famous literary critic, and Callimachus, author of the Pinakes.

The Pinakes was the first attempt by a scholar to list
all the literature known to the ancient world.   One hundred
and twenty papyrus rolls were required to record this "catalog" or bibliography.   Perhaps the next time you note a bibliography at the end of a chapter in a text book, you will remember that centuries ago Callimachus prepared a bibliography of world literature.

Other Greek scholars brought their imaginative ideas
to Alexandria.   Euclid, who made orderly the mathematics
of Pythagoras, presented his famous theories in The Elements
of Geometry, a manuscript translated and copied more than
any book except the Bible.

The science of astronomy--the secrets of the heavens
and an echo of the Wise Men and the Star--was widely practiced in Alexandria.   In 150 A.D. Claudius Ptolemy brought

to the scholars at Alexandria his model of the heavens in
which the sun and planets moved around the earth. Ptolemy's
theory survived for 1,400 years.

The destruction of the great Alexandrian library sig-
naled the Dark Ages in Europe. It was largely the spectacu-
lar strength of the Moslem Empire that kept learning alive.

The Destruction of the Library. In 47 B.C. Julius
Caesar fired the docks at Alexandria and, whether by mistake
or not, Brucheion was burned. Serapeum, which held the
overflow of rolls from Brucheion, then became the center of
learning and so continued until 391 A.D. when it was destroyed
by the Christians in their effort to do away with pagan literature.

It has been alleged that the Moslems, on their way to
the conquest of Europe, destroyed Serapeum. This idea is
questionable as the Moslems revered books and libraries.
If Serapeum had been in existence at the time the Moslems
were in Egypt, they would have been likely to cherish the
collection.

It is useless to expect archeologists to excavate the
ruins of Alexandria. The city lies below sea level and only
catacombs (cemeteries) and a few pillars have been sighted.
A rich but uncovered treasure is this buried city of Alexandria, with its half-million people, its library of a million
papyrus rolls and the tomb in which Alexander the Great is
said to lie, wrapped in gold.

THE LIBRARY AT PERGAMUM

Rivaling the Alexandrian library was the library at
Pergamum in Macedonia, Asia Minor. The king, Eumenes
II (197-159 B.C.), swore to build in his city of Pergamum
the most magnificent library in the ancient world.

The story is told that he tried to entice a librarian
from Alexandria to organize the collection. In retaliation,
the Egyptians placed an embargo on papyrus, thus depriving
Eumenes of writing material. Eumenes was not disturbed
and promptly invented parchment (pergamena) upon which to
copy the manuscripts. Scholars have exploded this myth,
contending that parchment had been used long before the time

of Eumenes. However, it was possible that parchment was manufactured in quantity at Pergamum and used as an item of trade.

German archeologists have excavated this city high on a hill top. Library rooms were found in the Temple of Athena. On the pavement lay broken a statue of the Goddess of Wisdom. Uncovered also were great columns that provided in ancient libraries a "walking and talking" space for scholars.

It is probable that the library contained about 110,000 rolls shelved in the pigeon-hole boxes. On the walls of the library rooms, the largest measuring 42 x 50 feet, holes were found which had probably been made for brackets to hold the shelving. The rolls were also stored in presses or cupboards similar to those used later in monastic libraries. On top of the press was placed the bust of the author whose works were stored in that particular press. These busts, found in the ruins, bore not only the name of the authors but the titles of the books they wrote.

Crates, the distinguished grammarian, served as a librarian at Pergamum. On a mission to Rome, he so praised the library and its collection of Greek classics that the Romans decided to "borrow" it. A Roman conqueror in 168 B.C. brought the library to Rome as part of the spoils of war. Later, Marc Antony is supposed to have given the rolls to Cleopatra to be added to the Alexandrian library. No authentic record verifies this gift.

In the restoration of the city of Pergamum archeologists enriched the history of ancient libraries.

ROMAN LIBRARIES

In the first 500 years of its existence Rome had no libraries. The Romans were too busy farming, building and colonizing to be concerned with learning. However, there came a realization of a glorious Greek culture across the Adriatic Sea that diminished the grandeur which was to be Rome.

The Romans were skillful borrowers and they set out to appropriate Greek culture--slaves, scholars, jewels, gold,

sculpture and libraries. One foray resulted in a parade on
the Roman streets of Perseus, the Greek hero, and a thousand Greek leaders in chains.   Well-educated Greeks were
forced to serve as teachers or were sent as scribes to the
East and to Alexandria to copy papyrus rolls.

Although the Romans were engineers, lawyers, and
politicians living in the midst of temples, forums and baths,
it now became the fashion to surround themselves with books
as a mark of social distinction.   The wealthy Romans displayed books in baths and in dining halls.   Greek household
slaves taught them to read.

Between 30 B. C. and 15 A. D. book shops filled an
entire street in Rome.   Scribes copied a book while the buy-
er waited.   Books were cheap, the equivalent of 15 to 50
cents in our money.

The book shop was a literary forum for browsing and
for dialogues on books and authors.   A list of new books was
posted on the door of the book shop.   Horace, the poet, and
the wit, Martial made the "best seller list" of those days.
Atticus gained fame as a Roman publisher.   Indeed, the Romans embraced culture as avidly as they had built and conquered.

Private Collections

Magnificent private libraries, luxurious rooms built
of green marble with rolls and codices in niches, presses,
decorated jars and bejeweled, purple leather capsae were the
proud possessions of scholars.   Marble busts of authors
adorned the presses.   Much time was spent on the care of
the papyrus and parchment rolls and codices, rolling, unrolling, glueing, trimming, smearing with cedar oil, fitting
covers and decorating knobs.

Cicero, with the aid of the publisher, Atticus, and the
scholar-slave Tyrannion, arranged in each of his 18 villas a
library room with painted shelves and a well-organized collection.

These private libraries and the influx of Greek "traveling libraries" awakened the Romans to the necessity of public libraries, available to all citizens.

Public Libraries

      Pollio, a patron of the poet, Virgil, made an unsuc-
cessful attempt in 39 B.C. to open a public library. As a
gesture of good will to the citizens of Rome, Julius Caesar
authorized the building of a public library but he was assas-
sinated before final plans were completed.

      Thirty-three years before Christ was born, the Em-
peror Augustus built a library and named it the Octaviana in
honor of his wife Octavia. The Octaviana was the most magnificent structure in Rome. Five years later Augustus built
another public library, the Palatine, on Palatine Hill. After
Nero burned Rome, a third public library, the Vespasian,
rose to prominence. These libraries were the first of 18
public libraries established in Rome.

      The Octaviana, the Palatine, the Vespasian and count-
less private libraries and great numbers of bookshops paved
the way for the Ulpiana.

      Erected by the Emperor Trajan in 98 A.D., the Ul-
piana stood near Trajan's Column. On this wondrous column
was carved a record of Trajan's victorious wars. The column still stands in the city of Rome. Archeologists, believing that the site of the Ulpiana was near the column, searched
in vain for some trace of the library. A plaque on a building near the column marks the supposed site.

      The Ulpiana was a scholar's library with well arranged
rolls and codices. Authors frequently mentioned in their writings the privilege of consulting materials in the collection.

      The physical features of Roman libraries, both public
and private, were similar. The buildings were of marble
with a double row of tall marble columns, open to the sky,
enclosing the entire area. This colonnade was used as a
"walking and talking" space for scholars. The pavement was
decorated with elaborate designs and crowded with bronze
statues of the gods.

      Within the confines of the columns were usually three
separate library buildings--one for Greek books, another for
Latin books, and a third housing the archives. The schola,
a school and lecture room, and a temple to the god who protected the library completed this elaborate library plan.

Within the library the rolls and codices were kept in pigeon-hole shelves and in presses with carved doors inlaid with ivory. The presses, usually built into the walls, had both vertical and horizontal shelves to accommodate the rolls and codices. The rolls were wrapped in linen, the more valuable ones covered with gaily dyed parchment. The walls of the library were painted and hung with sculptured portraits of authors. Benches for the convenience of the readers were placed near the shelves and presses.

The arrangement of books was simple. All the works of an author were kept together. Readers might consult two catalogs, one resembling a modern shelflist, the other an author catalog, giving the title, the first lines and brief biographical details.

Serving under a chief librarian, the Procurator Bibliothecarum, were assistant librarians, copyists and book binders.

The story of Roman libraries now draws to a close. By 400 A.D. the Vandals were plunging Rome into the Dark Ages. The libraries vanished. Fire, war, neglect and damp had ruined the rolls and codices. The splendid Roman library buildings had crumbled.

Undimmed by the shadow of Rome's fall, the four great libraries of antiquity endure as monuments of ancient culture: Assurbanipal's royal library at Ninevah; the Greek library at Alexandria on Egyptian soil; Pergamum, an archeological prize in Macedonia, and the magnificent Ulpiana built by Trajan in Rome.

Books and Libraries: Bridges to the Middle Ages

A few libraries existed beyond the borders of the city of Rome. At Athens, Hadrian built a most famous library. Preserved in the Vatican Library, Vatican City, are two busts of authors that once graced Hadrian's library. At Rhodes, in a school attended by wealthy Roman youths there was a distinguished collection of rolls. Fire destroyed the library gathered by the Emperors Constantine and Julian at Constantinople. Among the treasures burned was a manuscript of Homer, written on snake skin in letters of gold.

Excavated 150 years ago was the city of Herculaneum,

buried under volcanic ash in 79 A. D.   Three thousand
charred rolls in boxes have been miraculously restored and
deciphered.

The private library of a wealthy Roman was uncovered
in Egypt, 120 miles south of Cairo.   The collection may have
belonged to a member of a Christian colony that fled Rome
to escape persecution.   For 1,500 years the papyri, known
now as the Oxyrhynchus papyri, were preserved in the sand.
The contents of the collection were especially valuable as
fragments of early Christian writings, including the New
Testament, are rare finds.

In caves west of the Dead Sea, a religious group, the
Essenes, lived a monastic existence.   In 1947, a boy seeking a lost goat from his herd happened to spy earthen jars
in one of the caves.   Within the jars were thin copper sheets
and 600 rolls of papyri, probably from a scriptorium of the
Essenes order.   The find, known as the Dead Sea Scrolls,
has been the subject of bitter disputes and searching study.
Deciphered after an amazing restoration, the rolls were found
to contain parts of the Old Testament.

Christian libraries, especially those at Jerusalem and
Caesarea, were religious in content--the Gospels, sermons,
letters of the disciples and commentaries on the Scriptures.
The Church scorned pagan literature.   However, a few scholars kept pagan learning alive until the Church recovered its
senses and men like Cassiodorus built a bridge between pagan and Christian thought.

Learning and libraries now belonged to the monasteries.

CAUTIONARY SUGGESTIONS

"Not the fact avails, but the use you make of it,"
are the words of Ralph Waldo Emerson.

Why not make use of the facts in this chapter to
reach your own conclusions about the contribution of ancient
libraries to both the ancient and the modern world.

Ask your instructor to organize a discussion group.

Members of the group might include some students who have
read the chapter and some who have not.   In getting the discussion underway and to keep it rolling, the following questions might be useful:

I.   What contributions were made by ancient libraries to
     present day culture?

     Is the present an extension of the past and the future
     an awakening of the present?   In your opinion, does
     the past influence the present?

     What specific contributions did libraries make to the
     advancement of culture in Mesopotamia, Egypt, Greece
     and Rome?

     Which country most affected ancient culture--Greece
     or Rome?

     If libraries had not developed, what would have taken
     their place?

     What would a Babylonian king have scorned in our cul-
     ture?

II. Let's resort to science fiction.   The year is 5000
     A.D.   Archeologists from another planet are excavat-
     ing the dead city of New York.   What are they de-
     ducing from the headless lions that crouched in front
     of the New York Public Library, the bell tower of
     Riverside Church, the twisted rails of a subway line,
     a pile of illuminated manuscripts in the rubble of the
     Morgan Library, a computer in Rockefeller Center?
     How would our culture be interpreted?

III. Men of stature have usually dominated certain periods
     of culture.   Match the men of ancient times listed be-
     low with men in similar fields of endeavor today.

                    Yesterday   Today

                 Aristotle   _____
                 Callimachus   _____
                 Euripides   _____
                 Assurbanipal   _____
                 Crates   _____

Do you believe the distinguished men of ancient times
to have been more influential than their counterparts
today? What are the reasons for your decision.

TO INSTRUCT AND AMUSE

If you like to draw or sketch, make a floor plan of a
Roman library, including the great double row of columns
surrounding the area, the libraries, the schola, the temples
and the statuary. Color the pavement, and if you should de-
cide to label your sketch the Octaviana or the Palatine, add
a portico overlooking the Tiber River.

An archeologist's drawing of the restored Roman
Forum in an historical atlas will be of help to you.

If you like to look at pictures, then ask your librarian
for a book titled They Wrote on Clay by Edward Chiera.
The pictures in this delightful book may lead you to other
stories of archeological "finds."

Add to your collection of paperbacks a copy of The
Gold of the Gods by Erich Von Däniken. This book is prehistory, setting forth a strange, new theory of Earth and
the "era of the gods," based on a recent, archeological discovery.

In 1969 in Peru and Ecuador, South America, Juan
Moricz stumbled into miles and miles and miles of under-
ground tunnels that may date back to 15,000 B.C. To further astound and confound scientists and archeologists, the
claim is made that the tunnels were dug with a thermal
drill--which was supposed to have been invented for our as-
tronauts to use on the moon.

A "metal" library has been found in the tunnels. Two
to three thousand metal plaques, 32" x 1'7", stood on edge
like the pages of a book. On the plaques were cut unknown
characters. Writing?

Later chapters in the Von Däniken book tell of other
unusual "digs" and "finds" around the world.

Certain scholars laugh at the author's off-the-beaten-
track ideas. Will you?

FURTHER READING

Kenyon, Frederic C. Books and Readers in Ancient Greece
    and Rome. 2d ed. Oxford: Clarendon Press, 1951.
        Gives you the feeling that "you are there" in the
ancient libraries of Athens and Rome. A few pictures.

Parsons, Edward Alexander. The Alexandrian Library,
    Glory of the Hellenic World; Its Rise, Antiquities and
    Destructions. Amsterdam: Elsevier Press, 1952.
        Not for the casual reader, but you will recognize a
host of names and places, from Cleopatra to Callimachus,
from Brucheion to Pergamum.

Richardson, Ernest Cushing. The Beginnings of Libraries.
    Hamden, Conn.: Archon Books, 1963.
        Author of several books on ancient libraries, Richard-
son dramatizes his facts. Easy to read.

Thompson, James Westfall. Ancient Libraries. Berkeley:
    University of California Press, 1940.
        A brief and clear story about early libraries. Writ-
ten by a distinguished historian.

Chapter 4

THE MONKS COPY AND COPY AND COPY

"Keepers of books, keepers
also of the human spirit"
--Archibald MacLeish

Seated at wooden benches, copying over and over with
cramped fingers, the monks strove to preserve the records
of Christian culture. As the mighty Roman civilization moved
to an end, the monks held a light, flickering and dim, but a
light from the past for the future.

AS THE DARK AGES CAME

With the fall of Rome, the ancient world belonged to
history. In the half-century before 285 A.D., 18 Roman
emperors reigned. Sixteen were slain. Violence led to more
violence as the Romans, losing their desire for military conquest, became distrustful of the misused power of their
armies. Values in literature and the arts and regard for a
code of laws dipped low.

Disorder and confusion made it possible in 312 A.D.
for Constantine the Great to overcome the Roman army at
Milvian Bridge. Before the battle Constantine had a vision
of a huge cross in the sky. Thereupon he ordered his soldiers to make their shields with this Christian symbol--Chi-
Rho. Their battle cry was, "By this sign we conquer."
And they did.

Emperor Constantine sheltered the Christian church.
He prohibited pagan rites, suppressed the bloody combats of
gladiators and, instead of temples to the gods, built churches.

Later, in a further extension of his Empire, Constantine
looked to the East. Here, in the most beautiful harbor on
the Mediterranean, he fashioned a new city in the image of
Rome and named it Constantinople. In 330 A.D. Constantine
founded the Imperial Library, devoted to Roman and Greek
classics and Christian writings. The library, in spite of
fires and censorship, was culturally important for 1000 years.
Manuscripts from it were copied in the monasteries of the
West, influencing a new birth of learning, the Renaissance.

Gradually the culture of the Roman Empire moved
from pagan to Christian. The church was not yet strong
enough to prevail. Violence flared again. Pagan life became glutted and misdirected. Gone were the early Roman
virtues of courage, industry and pride in their country.
Scholarship was at a low ebb. Libraries were closed and
books destroyed.

THE LAST OF THE ROMAN SCHOLARS

During this time of turmoil it is possible that all
classical literature might have disappeared without the dedicated work of a few pagan scholars such as Boethius and
Cassiodorus.

Boethius, the last of the aristocratic Romans, pursued learning and truth for its own sake. He wrote on
arithmetic, music, astronomy and translated Plato and Aristotle. His Confessions is considered a literary classic.
Boethius died a Christian martyr, believing that only God
can satisfy man's search for happiness.

Cassiodorus, a scholar and a contemporary of Boethius,
fled Rome after sieges and captures. He founded a monastery and within it organized a library and a school. He
trained the monks to copy pagan and Christian works, believing that "the devil should be fought with pen and ink."

Cassiodorus was a careful transcriber, setting forth
in a number of books instructions for the copying of manuscripts. He produced samples of the proper bindings of
manuscripts and in his writing room provided sun dials and
water clocks for telling time and lanterns for copying after
dark.

Cassiodorus wrote a monumental History of the Goths. Unfortunately the manuscript was either lost or destroyed. Its preservation would have given historians a true picture of the invasions of the barbarians from the north, a much debated epoch of ancient history.

THE RISE OF THE MONASTERIES

To escape persecution as Christians, and to avoid the wickedness of the city, men fled to the hills and to the loneliness of hidden caves.

These men, called hermits or anchorites, organized into communities. Thus were the monasteries originated to protect the monks, bound by vows of chastity, obedience and poverty.

The monks were tillers of the soil, vinegrowers and herdsmen. They glorified hard and honorable labor; observed faithfully their religious practices; cared for the sick and the poor, and organized monastic schools for boys. By copying and copying manuscripts, they spread the Christian faith and preserved the final vestiges of Greek and Roman culture.

FOUNDERS OF MONASTIC ORDERS

Leaders from scattered groups of hermits and anchorites organized them into monastic communities. In 250 A.D. the first monastic community was established by St. Pachomius, a hermit who fled to the edge of the Egyptian desert and gathered about him other hermits. Each lived alone in a separate hut, meeting daily for prayers and instruction. St. Pachomius, believing that a monastic community must maintain itself, taught the hermits basket weaving, blacksmithing and tailoring. This principle of community living became the first monastic rule.

St. Basil of the Quiet Hand

In the East, the Christian bishops were alarmed at the emergence of a group of pseudo-monks who resorted to fearful penances--one sat for 35 years on a pillar, others

inflicted self-punishment by beating themselves with chains
until the blood ran. St. Basil, a church father, a writer
and a man of action, quelled these outrageous customs and
directed the monks to work in the fields, to weave baskets
and to help the poor and the sick. A rule was established
and a monastery built--a pattern for other monastic orders
in the East.

St. Benedict, a Man of Vision

The "father of monasticism" was St. Benedict. As
a wealthy, young man he was sent to Rome to study. Horri-
fied by the excesses of the government, he fled to Subiaco
where he lived as a hermit in a cave, drawing like-minded
young men around him by his charm and holiness. One of
his followers plotted to poison him, whereupon St. Benedict
fled to Monte Cassino on the road to Naples.

After demolishing a pagan temple St. Benedict built a
great monastery on the site. The story is told of workmen
who tried again and again to dislodge a huge stone that inter-
fered with the building of a wall. St. Benedict was sum-
moned. Over the stone he made the sign of the Cross. The
stone moved.

The monastery, named after the village over which it
towered, was the most influential one in Europe. From it
the Benedictine monks journeyed to found new monasteries
and to spread St. Benedict's simple and enduring creed that
work brings bodily and spiritual health.

Through the centuries Monte Cassino was destroyed
by fire, rebuilt, ravished by neglect and again restored.
What was thought to be its final destruction occurred in World
War II. The Germans, during the invasion of Italy, stored
in the cellars of the monastery vast quantities of ammunition.
As the Allies marched toward Monte Cassino, this great
building was destroyed by "German fury. " A small portion
of one wall was left standing. American money rebuilt Monte
Cassino. Carefully preserved was a small portion of the
original wall.

St. Benedict wrote the Regula, a practical guide to
life in the ordered existence of a religious house. In the
Regula was set forth for the monks the rule of their lives:
their vows; prayers and time of prayers; their work in the

fields, raising grain, grapes and sheep; a time to read and
to learn Latin and Greek; a time for sleep and food; a time
to care for the sick; and above all, according to Rule 48, a
time to copy manuscripts. The powerful influence of St.
Benedict, who in turn had been influenced by Cassiodorus,
led other leaders to take pride in the monastery as a center
of learning. The Benedictine monks were preservers and
teachers of classical and Christian culture, and regulated
their lives under the code of St. Benedict, who truly believed that "by the sweat of thy brow thou shalt eat bread."

St. Columba, the Glory of the Written Word

From a monastery in the heather-covered uplands of
Iona, in the Hebrides, St. Columba set out with 28 monks to
bring the Christian faith to the Britons and to the continent
of Europe. He and his monks claimed to have stablished 28
monasteries, a monk being left to organize a rule in each
new house.

Greater, however, than his missionary zeal was St.
Columba's desire to copy each and every manuscript he could
beg, borrow or steal, and his emphasis of the importance of
studying and copying as a monastic duty.

In beautiful script, he copied manuscripts like a
thirsty traveler gulping a bowl of cold water. It is said that
he made 300 copies of the Psalter and the Gospels. Whether
St. Columba left the copy and took the original manuscript is
not known, but legends galore have gathered about his name.

A story is told of his desire to copy a manuscript
that decorated the altar of a monastic chapel. The Abbot of
the monastery refused St. Columba's request. In the black
of night, he crept to the altar and, guided by a mysterious
light emanating from the palm of his hand, copied the manuscript.

Yet another tale is told of an abbot who would not al-
low St. Columba to copy a precious and prized manuscript
which was jealously guarded. Disappointed, St. Columba
hurled a curse on the manuscript. At vespers, the manuscript was opened for the reading of a prayer. The writing
was so scrambled that it could not be deciphered. It is also
claimed that when the curse was delivered, all the book
satchels in the monastery fell of their hooks onto the ground.

Legends about St. Columba reveal his faith in the
glory of the written word. In his exquisite Celtic uncial hand
is preserved in the Royal Irish Academy, Dublin, a fragment
of a 6th century Cathach, the earliest surviving speciman of
Celtic capital letters.

St. Augustine--Forty Monks and Nine Books

Accompanied by 40 monks, St. Augustine was sent
from Rome to Christianize the Britons. At Canterbury, in
a desolate fen, he established a monastery, which became
the mother-school of England.

St. Augustine brought from Rome nine precious manuscripts. Among them was a Bible with leaves painted rose
and purple; two Psalters bearing silver images of Christ,
and the Gospels on which a countryman swore an oath falsely
and is said to have lost his sight. None of these manuscripts
is extant. They were copied and read "to pieces."

St. Francis and St. Dominic, Mendicant Monks

Late in monastic history, the Franciscans and Dominicans led by St. Francis and St. Dominic of Spain became
known as mendicant or begging friars. The Dominicans were
teachers and preachers. The Franciscans possessed nothing,
no shelter, no money, their lives devoted to outcasts, lepers
and the poor.

St. Francis was a singer of songs. To his father's
disgust he spurned combat and became a singer of the love
of God for man. Retold many times are remarkable tales
of his understanding of the language of birds and wild beasts.

The Franciscan monks made only a small contribution
as scholars, but they did spread the joy and hope of the
Christian faith.

THE MONASTERY BUILDING

The traditional image of the monk who spent his days
at prayer comes to us from very early medieval times. So,
too, does the image of the cold, stone building known as the

monastery. Shutting out the world, the walls were built a-
round a hollow square known as the close. Encircling the
close, the cloisters hugged the building, their arches open
to the sky. Here the monks walked and read their offices.
Here, too, in box-like carrels they copied manuscripts.
Seated on hard, wooden benches, often in bitter weather, they
struggled to see in the dim light, a manuscript spread on a
high lectern. It is small wonder that one monk wrote on
the margin of his copy, "O, for a glass of wine."

The monastery usually contained a chapel with simple
altar fittings, including an antiphonary and a precious service
book in a decorated cover.

In the chapter house the secular business of the monastery was conducted. Manuscripts were copied and stored
in a room of the chapter house known as the scriptorium.
Other rooms in the monastery were the refectory, or dining
hall, the infirmary, the winery, and cell-like sleeping spaces
for the monks.

Privileged monks, who held offices in the monastic
order were: the porter who guarded the gate; the armarius
or librarian; the almoner, who cared for the poor and the
sick; the cellarer, in charge of wine making; and the Abbot,
the traditional leader of the monastic group.

THE SCRIPTORIUM

If a monastic scribe were to enter a modern library,
he would no doubt drop his goose quill pen in astonishment.
The size, the color, the light and warmth, the books stacked
on shelves from floor to ceiling, the comfortable chairs, the
cabinets of art objects, the audio-visual hardware, the magazines spread on the tables would be beyond his comprehension.
Possibly the only thing he might recognize would be a sign
reading Silence, providing it was written in Latin.

His library-writing room, known as the scriptorium,
was either a part of the chapter house or was built over it,
with neither heat nor artificial light. The stone floors were
strewn with straw for warmth; the windows were set small
and low in stone walls; the furniture consisted of rude benches
and slanted desks known as lecterns. The book presses which
stood against the wall or were recessed into the wall held

supplies and the manuscripts which had been copied. The
book presses were roughly built, wooden cupboards with
shelves and double doors which could be secured. Later book
presses were delicately and gracefully designed with carved
doors and metal ornaments.

Book chests were also used for storing the manuscripts
In the early Celtic monasteries, rough leather satchels with
long leather handles were hung on wooden pegs on the walls
of the writing room. The satchels were also used as carrying cases by the monks as they journeyed in search of manuscripts to copy.

In the scriptorium was preserved what had been written in order that more might be written.

THE ARMARIUS

A learned monk, the armarius or librarian, was in
charge of the scriptorium. His duties were many and varied.
An exact record had to be kept of all manuscripts in the
presses, and the manuscripts guarded against soil, theft and
mutilation. If the manuscript collection was to increase in
numbers, then the Armarius must seek from other monasteries manuscripts to copy. This often entailed long and
dangerous journeys. He also assigned to each monk a daily
task. Gathering and distributing supplies was an important
duty: awls for holding down the parchment, leads for ruling
the pages, pen knives for erasures, pumice for smoothing
rough spots in the parchment, and goose and turkey quill
pens had to be sharpened. A most important duty was the
preparation of ink and parchment.

Medieval recipes for the making of inks are found frequently in manuscripts. Black ink was made from gall nuts,
a growth on the bark and leaves of the oak tree. The nuts
were soaked in wine and strained through a cloth. A cop-
peras solution was added and mixed with flour and gum or
resin. The mixture was either poured into a container or
shaped into a "tablet" which the monks wrapped in cloth and
placed under their pillows in order to maintain a soft con-
sistency. Water was added to the "tablet" before copying.
The black ink went onto the parchment very pale, but grew
blacker with time.

The making of the glorious colored inks for illuminating the manuscripts was a mysterious process. It is ex-
plained in detail for you in De Arte Illumandi, a 14th century
treatise on the technique of manuscript illumination. Note
the formula for making violet ink from the flowers of the
violet plant. Ask your librarian to borrow the book for you.

The procedure for making the parchment used in the
copying of manuscripts was uncomplicated but the quantity of
parchment needed made it an arduous task. One codex
might require the skins of 200 sheep. The method of making
parchment is described in chapter 2.

The armarius also proofread the work of each scribe
and corrected his many errors. If the day's task of all the
scribes was to copy the same page of a manuscript, then the
armarius dictated the Latin text.

He was also responsible for "order" in the scriptorium
and utter silence was maintained as the monks labored at
their benches and lecterns. The armarius was highly regarded as a scholar and his tasks in the scriptorium were
important ones.

THE MONKS AS SCRIBES

The copying of libri manu scripti (books written by
hand) was a constant and never-ending task of monastic
scribes. They copied only during daylight hours, averaging
six hours each day. It was hard work. A monk wrote in
the margin of the manuscript he was copying, "Writing is
drudgery. It crooks your back, it dims your sight and
twists your stomach and your sides." An added burden was
the Latin language, which was unfamiliar to some of the
monks.

It was not uncommon for a monk to copy only 400
pages in a year's time. However, he believed that for each
word copied a sin would be forgiven on Judgment Day.

Since the scribes had to work in silence, gestures
were used to communicate. If a sacred work was being
copied and questions arose concerning the transcribing, the
scribe made the sign of the Cross to summon the armarius.
For guidance in copying a pagan work, the scribe scratched

behind his ear like a dog. (Pagans were called "dogs" even
as some of our minority groups are unhappily nicknamed today.)

The Creation of the Monastic Manuscript

        The actual process of copying demanded considerable
preparation. When a scribe received the sheets of parchment, the sheets were folded once in a folio and were in
proper order; that is, recto--front or flesh side of the parchment, and verso--back or hair side. Using awls, the scribe
fastened the parchment to the slant-top desk because parchment has a tendency to curl. Then, with a blunt lead stick,
the scribe drew faint vertical marginal lines and horizontal
lines to carry the text. These lines left furrows on the
verso of the page, thus making it easier for scholars to re-
assemble a manuscript, as no pagination was used. Sufficient
space was left on the page so that the rubricator or illuminator might embellish the page with red and blue letters or
ornamental historiated initials. The binders them assembled
the pages and, for protection, added a cover of roughly tanned
leather. The book then became the cherished possession of
a monastery or it might be presented as a gift to royalty.

        When the size and style of the letters were determined,
the scribe, to save time, used abbreviations. These were
designated by a bar over the word; for example, $\overline{dms}$ for
dominus, $\overline{Sp}$ for Spiritus and $\overline{X}$ for Christus. As a gentle
reminder when you send a Christmas greeting, write, Merry
$\overline{X}$mas.

        As the manuscript was completed, the scribe sighed
with relief and added a colophon, which might be a prayer
for God's blessing on the work or a curse on him who tried
to soil or steal the manuscript. Sometimes the colophon
bore a humorous line or two such as, "This book is done.
'Tis time I think. To give the scribe some cash for drink. "
Or, "Three fingers hold the pen but the whole body toils.
Thanks be to God. "

        Scholars, however, as they attempt to date an early
manuscript, are most grateful to a monk who wrote a colophon in this manner: "Done this 12th day of the first month
of the year 1032 A. D. by me, Brother John, at the order of
the Abbot of Tours for the salvation of his soul. Pray God
my sins forgiven. " The colophon, in time, became the title
page.

Thus the monastic scribes copied.   What did they
copy?

The Nature and Content of the Treasures Copied

Copied over and over so many times that the scribes
knew it "by heart" was the Bible.   The translation by St.
Jerome of the Greek Bible into the Latin, or Vulgate, was
the common source.

The Psalters or Psalms were a favorite assignment.
This majestic poetry gave flight to the scribes' monotonous
copying and heightened the art of the rubricator and illuminator.

Service books, prayers, hymns, sermons, missals,
breviaries, commentaries on the Bible, and lives of Saints
were copied and recopied.   Used by the canons and the entire choir was the great antiphon the music of the Mass.   A
four-line staff and square notes graced the antiphonary, which
was copied in high-pointed letters and imaginatively rubricated.

The Books of Hours were manuscripts illuminated with
splendid color and skill.   They contained the Office of the
Virgin, prayers, poetry and full-page paintings depicting medieval life and times.   These beautiful Hour Books are often
on display in libraries and museums.   Buy a facsimile for
your own library as a constant reminder of the monks who
copied and copied and copied.

At this point you may have concluded that the monks
copied only religious materials.   As monastic schools grew,
a Latin grammar known as a donatus was in demand.   A few
secular manuscripts were also copied largely for compara-
tive studies of paganism and Christianity.

In the 15th century the copying and illuminating of
manuscripts was usually done by paid scribes and artists.

The monasteries had lost their power and influence,
their work usurped by an agrarian society, by the rise of the
universities and by the invention of printing.

In England, Henry VIII confiscated the monasteries.
Those remaining on the Continent focused largely on the re-

ligious life, often maintaining themselves in isolation and silence.

In the story of books and libraries honor must be
given to the monks who labored in the scriptoria. Compared
to the modern, computerized printing press, their method of
producing hand-written books appears primitive indeed, but in
copying, preserving and extending a body of literature they
provided a bridge from the Dark Ages to modern civilization.

A SUMMARY

Do the following statements summarize what you have
learned in this chapter?

The fall of Rome led to a period in history known as
the Dark Ages. A few pagan and Christian scholars kept the
ancient culture alive until the rise of the monasteries.

Hermits and anchorites fleeing from the turmoil in
Rome were gathered by strong, like-minded men into communities. Under the guidance of such leaders as St. Benedict, Cassiodorus, St. Columba and St. Augustine, the communities grew into monastic orders.

The monks, under vows of chastity, poverty and obedience, glorified work, practiced their Christian devotions,
founded schools and, by the copying of manuscripts, preserved classical culture and extended Christian learning.

With its high walls shutting out the world, the monastery made possible a well-ordered religious existence. The
chapter house with a scriptorium and a school, the chapel,
infirmary, refectory, winery and cells for the monks re-
sembled a medieval town.

The Bible, service books and Latin grammars were
patiently copied, rubricated and illuminated by the monks.
A small number of secular books were copied. Parchment,
quill pens, ink, a lectern and desk were their "printing
presses." Copying was no mean task.

The late Middle Ages witnessed the downfall of the
monasteries. The universities demanded greater numbers of

books, especially in the sciences.   Printing by movable type
swept through Europe like a fire.   The "Renaissance man"
was already searching for a new world!   The work of the
monastic scribe was nearly done--but his contribution was
beyond measure.

GROUP ACTIVITIES

You and your friends might discover in the life and
times of St. Columba lively background material for the writing of a prize-winning one-act play for a Spring Drama Fes-
tival or a TV documentary.   An artistic setting at rugged
Iona, a dramatic and versatile leading character, St. Columba, simple but effective costuming, easy dialogue and music
sung by the bards would challenge and intrigue a talented
group of young people.

Visit a local book store and examine facsimiles of
the wondrous Books of Hours.   Why not buy one?   For example, the Hours of Catherine of Cleves would delight you
and your friends.   Put it on display in the school library.

Ask your librarian for a catalog of filmstrips or
search the card catalog for visual materials on monasteries,
monastic leaders and monastic scribes.   Suggest the films
be shown in your classroom.

Here is a most ambitious and most rewarding project.
It begins with the purchase of the skin of a sheep from which
a sheet of parchment is made according to directions given
in chapter 2.   Inks, black and colored, are concocted from
recipes in De Arte Illumandi.   With a turkey quill, a page
of a medieval manuscript is copied in the manner of the monastic scribes, using abbreviations and supplying a colophon.
A great historiated initial, containing an appropriate picture,
a border--either geometric or a realistic design--and red
and blue rubricated capitals are added with help of the Art
department.

The completed manuscript can be a center of a library display.   The project might be of interest to other students.   It might be fun, too.

FURTHER READING

Diringer, David.   The Hand-produced Book.   New York:
     Philosophical Library, 1953.
          Clearly, carefully and thoroughly explained in this
detailed account of the book in the making.   Pictures contribute much to the text, each page being filled with things
to learn about the hand-produced book.

Fremantle, Anne.   Age of Faith.   New York: Time-Life,
     c. 1965.
          Beautiful pictures, many in color, tell the story of
medieval days from a religious viewpoint.   Note the chapter
on "Communities of Pious Brethren," especially the pictures
of the chapter house and "Fighting the Devil by Pen and Ink. "

Thompson, David Varney, ed.   De Arte Illumandi, Technique
     of Manuscript Illumination.   New Haven: Yale University
     Press, 1933.
          A curious 14th century pamphlet with descriptions of
the preparation of the materials for writing in the monastic
scriptorium.

Thompson, James Westfall.   The Medieval Library.   New
     York: Hafner, 1957.
          The chapter dealing with the monastic scriptorium
(writing room) will increase your appreciation of the diffi-
culties encountered by the monks as they copied and copied.
The first place to turn for a description of a scriptorium.

Chapter 5

THE MANUSCRIPT LIGHTED UP

"A thing of beauty is a joy forever."
--John Keats

In the long history of the book, the illuminated manuscript of the Middle Ages stands alone in glory. Words cannot impart the beauty of the soft, grey-white vellum; the perfectly formed letters; the ornamental borders, some resembling a flower or vegetable garden; and the huge historiated initials, a riot of colors coupled with gold and silver, lighted up the manuscripts.

No novice can be expected to examine an illuminated manuscript and identify the century in which a monk bent over each stroke in a letter and the rubricator and illuminator lavished their art. Nor can the novice discern the school of illumination to which the manuscript might belong, or determine the manner in which gold was laid on or colors mixed. Scholars have spent lifetimes of study and written volumes on the identification, location and characteristics of a vast number of illuminated manuscripts.

While it must be left to the scholars to describe an illuminated manuscript in such detail as Lectionary and Vita S Benedicti, Vat. Lat. 1202, fol. 2r, the novice can do more than characterize an illuminated manuscript as "pretty."

APPRECIATION OF THE MANUSCRIPT

To understand the artistry of the illuminated manuscript, you need to:

Appreciate that the medieval mind loved color and lavished this love on illuminated manuscripts with colors both delicate and blazing, silver and gold.

Recognize that the illuminated manuscript was a religious expression, a part of the glorification of churches with their frescoes, mosaics and stained glass.

Identify the historiated initial (an initial letter always containing a picture within it).

Realize that from the initial letter gentle and increasingly complicated designs ran down the margin, extending around the page and finally exploding into a magnificent border.

Note that in some illuminated manuscripts there are pages filled with intricate, almost unbelievable geometric designs or full-page panel paintings with magnificent color and artistry.

Establish a time sequence for the illuminated manuscript, which rose at the beginning of the Middle Ages in the 6th century, reached its glory in the 14th and 15th centuries, and died with the invention of printing.

Recognize the types of manuscripts which were usually illuminated, such as: prayer books; the Old and the New Testament; missals or Mass books; breviaries, the priest's service books; Psalters, the Psalms; books about animals, bestiaries; antiphons, huge music books from which the choir read the Mass; and elegant Books of Hours. These manuscripts contained prayers for the services of the day; a calendar or poems were usually a gift book for a King, a Queen, a Court favorite, a patron of the arts.

Know that often a manuscript was named for the monastery in which it was produced, e.g., the Book of Durrow; for the library that housed it, such as the Vatican Virgil; or for the person to whom the manuscript belonged, as Queen Mary's Psalter.

With an appreciation of these qualities of an illuminated manuscript, you need no longer comment, "How pretty." You can now comment intelligently: There's an historiated initial! This manuscript is decorated with intricate geometric designs!

This is an antiphonary! The Vatican Virgil?--it must be named
for the Vatican Library where it is housed.

SCHOOLS OF ILLUMINATION

Scholars have classified illuminated manuscripts under
schools of illumination: Classical, Celtic, Byzantine, Carolingian, English, French, Italian, Flemish. Characteristics
of the schools are in some cases pronounced, as in the geometric designs of the Celtic School, the diapering of the
English School, or the white line of the Italian School.

But an identification of certain manuscripts by school
is possible only after considerable study, and scholars delight in disputes over whether a manuscript is of the Early
English School with Celtic and Carolingian borrowings, or
Carolingian with Celtic and Byzantine borrowings.

As an added dividend to the appreciation of the beauty
of an illuminated manuscript, you can purchase a facsimile
(copy) of an illuminated manuscript (some can be obtained for
as little as two dollars) and study the hand writing, the great
initials, the borders, the miniatures (small pictures without
the use of gold), the panel paintings and wonder at the
sources of the marvelous color. When and where was the
manuscript copied and embellished? Where is the original
manuscript--in a national library, a museum, or privately
owned? Perhaps you will promise yourself some day to see
the original of your facsimile as well as other beautiful manuscripts from the rich legacy of the Middle Ages.

You may then agree with Falconer Madan, who wrote:

> Even the red rubrics, the plain blue and red let-
> ters ... relieve the eye; but when capital letters
> are floriated, when the margins are filled with leaf-
> and-branch work, and when every few pages exhibit
> a delicately painted miniature ... we feel that the
> accessories have invested the written page with a
> beauty and attractiveness beyond the power of a
> scribe alone. *

*Falconer Madan. Books in Manuscript, a Short Introduction
to Their Study and Use. 2d ed., rev. London, 1920.

SIX FAMOUS MANUSCRIPTS

Which of the hundreds of illuminated manuscripts would you wish to see with your own eyes? Six are chosen here as exemplifying the early and the late, the beginning and the ending of the glorious illuminated manuscript of medieval times.

The Cottonian Genesis

Scholars might insist that either the Vatican Virgil or the Vienna Genesis, which is also in the Vatican Library, be chosen as an example of the early illuminated manuscript rather than the Cottonian Genesis. Perhaps rightly, as the Cottonian Genesis is no longer a great codex with illuminated pages, but only a few charred fragments, 150 pieces, laid out on paper in the British Museum.

The library of Sir Robert Cotton at Ashburnham burned, and nearly all of his precious manuscripts were destroyed. This destruction is a reminder of how fragile is the life of a manuscript. Fire, flood, "travels" from one monastery to another for copying, thieves, who hid the manuscript where it was subject to neglect and decay, were among the hazards threatening the preservation of manuscripts.

The Cottonian Genesis is a Septuagint (in Greek) of parts of the Bible. It was copied in the 5th century in inch-high, rounded capital letters, called uncials, and adorned with 250 paintings in water colour. The pictures were the same width as the text and usually at the bottom of the page with a few lines of text above. Each pictures with its blue background was enclosed in bands of red, black, white and pale yellow. Particularly realistic were the nature scenes depicted in the drawings.

Like many other manuscripts, the Cottonian Genesis "traveled." It was brought from Macedonia by two Greek bishops as a gift for King Henry VIII of England. He gave it to his daughter, Elizabeth I, who in turn gave it to her tutor, Sir John Fortescue. He placed it in the library of Sir Robert Cotton. What is left of it is now in the British Museum.

The Lindisfarne Gospels

This magnificent manuscript was copied and decorated

at the monastery of Lindisfarne in Northumbria. The monastery, founded by the Celtic monks of Iona, was a meeting
place of the cultures of the Celts and of the monks sent from
Rome to christianize England.

Two hundred and fifty-eight pages contain the text of
the four Gospels written by the four Evangelists, Matthew,
Mark, Luke and John. Copied and illuminated between 698-
721 A.D., the manuscript is a treasure of the British Museum where it is known as the Book of Lindisfarne.

Even with a magnifying glass, it is almost impossible
to follow the marvelous precision and minuteness of the geometric patterns. The five cruciform pages depicting forms
of the Cross have never been surpassed in workmanship.
Portraits of the four Evangelists and the Canon tables (church
law) written within stately arches are elaborately executed.
The colors are mild and beautifully blended, blue, green,
dark red, mauve, purple, yellow and pink.

Other manuscripts done in the style of the Lindisfarne
Gospels are the Book of Durrow and the Codex Amiatinus.
The Book of Durrow is in the Trinity College Library, Dublin
and has a colophon stating that it was copied by St. Columba.
Known as Codex A, the Codex Amiatinus is housed in the li-
brary of Lorenzo de Medici, the Laurentian, in Florence,
Italy. Sent as a gift to the Pope in Rome, Codex A was
copied and illuminated in the Northumbrian monasteries.

But the Book of Kells, done at about the same time
as the Lindisfarne Gospels is considered the finest manuscript
ever produced--to be counted among the wonders of the world.

The Book of Kells

Copied about 800 A.D. in the monasteries of Iona and
Kells, the Book of Kells has for the last 800 years been in
the Trinity College Library, Dublin. It is kept in a special
display case and one page is turned each day to protect the
colors from the light. Tourists and scholars visit the library
day after day in the hope that they will see the most beautiful page of all--the "XPI" page.

St. Columba and the "Book." Iona, an island off the
western coast of Scotland, sheltered at an early time a band
of Celtic monks. St. Columba came to his island in 563 A.D.

and under his devoted and inspired leadership the copying of
the great Book of Kells began.

He and his monks lived in rude, beehive-shaped cells.
The stone foundation, stone supports for a table, a seat and
a socket for a Cross have been uncovered by archeologists.
In one of these cells St. Columba slept on the bare, grey
rock. A small abbey church was built and walls were erect-
ed for defense. Parts of the wall still survive. Two carved
granite Crosses have stood there for 1,200 years. Blown
down by gales and broken, the Crosses have been partly restored.

St. Columba was buried in the Abbey church at Iona.
The graves of Duncan and Macbeth are said to be nearby.

The life story of a manuscript is often filled with
strange adventures. When the Vikings raided Iona, the monks
and their precious books fled to the monastery of Kells--
hence the name, Book of Kells.

The manuscript was kept in a golden casket, or cum-
dach. In 1006 A.D. the casket was stolen. The thief kept
the gold and hid the manuscript. But it was found by the
monks "under a sod." Two hundred years later the book
passed into the hands of Gerald Plunkett, and from him to
J. Ussher who gave it to the Trinity College Library in
Dublin.

The Copying and Painting. The Book of Kells
was copied in a beautifully clear, half-uncial script onto
730 leaves of glazed vellum made from the hides of at least
90 animals. Included are the four Gospels, portraits of the
Evangelists, Cruciform and Canon tables, the contents being
much like those of the Lindisfarne Gospels. The painting of
the Evangelists is crude. The eyes are oval discs, the hair
like skeins of yarn. The feet, with toes turned out, are
painted white, as are the hands. In a portrait of the Virgin
holding on her lap the Christ Child, the Child is grotesque
and almost as large as the Virgin. But the portraits were
surrounded by borders so full of an intricate chain of ornamentation as to be almost inconceivable. In one-fourth of a
square inch, 158 intertwining lines have been counted--they
"must have been traced by angels," someone said.

It is on the page at the opening of each Gospel that
the most lavish ornamentation occurs. The initial letter al-

most disappears under the twisting and turning of spirals, dots, three-spoked wheels, zig-zags, squares, elongated animals with tails in their mouths and with human heads.

Considered the most beautiful and elaborate page in the Book of Kells is the Khu-Rho, popularly known as the XPI page. So full of minute designs is this page that there is room left for only two Latin words of the text. Thirteen human-headed animals can be counted, and in the bottom left corner is a cat watching mice nibbling on the Eucharistic bread. The colors are reddish-brown, yellow and bluish-purple. No gold was used in the Book of Kells.

As superb as is this manuscript in its glory of color and calligraphy, the art of making books in Ireland was well known before the Book of Kells was copied. Preserved in the library of the Royal Irish Academy, Dublin, where it is occasionally on display is the Cathlac, a Psalter of the 6th century. Another ancient Irish manuscript was the Book of Durrow, produced 150 years before the Book of Kells.

From the bleak monastery at Iona came a wondrous work of art, but in the palaces and Courts of France emerged quite another type of the illuminated manuscript--the Books of Hours.

Les Très Riches Heures du Duc de Berry

This manuscript on vellum was done for the prince of French medieval book collectors, the Duc de Berry, by the brothers Limbourg. The names of these artists are significant. In earlier manuscripts the illuminator is usually unknown. However, the records of the Duc's rare manuscripts, jewels and art objects disclosed that the Limbourgs were salaried members of the Duc's household.

De Berry's collection of manuscripts was extensive, as evidenced by a catalog of his library. The British Museum and the Bibliothèque Nationale, Paris, own several of the Duc's manuscripts, but the treasure, the Très Riches Heures is in the Condé Museum at Chantilly, France.

This Book of Hours followed the usual pattern set for the contents of hundreds of medieval Hour Books: the Office of the Virgin, Psalms and prayers to the Saints.

    The Calendar Pages. The most appealing pages are
the calendar pages--one page for each month of the year.
The pictures on these pages are worth more than hundreds of
words written about life in the Middle Ages. Historians call
the pictures "social documents. "

    The calendar page for January in the Très Riches
Heures depicts the Duc at table, attended by his Court, his
knights in full armour, mounted and on foot; his priest; his
hunting dog. A feast table is set with a royal service of
gold plates, bowls and pitchers and on the walls hang colorful banners.

    February is shown as a month of snow--a town, the
woods around it covered with frost. In a walled farmyard
are beehives; granaries; a sheep fold; the hungry birds; a
farm wagon; a laborer leading a donkey loaded with faggots;
and a rude shed, the walls hung with hanks of drying yarn.
Around a blazing fire are the farm women warming their
legs, their voluminous skirts pulled up to their knees.

    March is portrayed as the month for sowing. A
farmer is plowing with a two-wheeled wooden plow drawn by
oxen. Other laborers bend over the rough furrows, planting
seeds. In a distant field a shepherd and his dog watch the
sheep. Roads around the field converge in an open space
where stands a shrine with a pointed spire. Shining in the
sun is a great castle with towers, pennants flying, a court-
yard, a moat and a high, white wall. It is presumed that
the castle belonged to the Duc de Berry. Above each calendar page, two vast arches, like rainbows in the sky, bear
signs of the Zodiac with the Sun God rampant.

    The Artistry of Color. The colors in the Très Riches
Heures are of surpassing beauty--clean, glowing colors that
have been applied with skill; brilliant blues flecked with golden
patterns; smoky, somber blues; flashing crimson in royal
robes; bright red in a hat or hunting jacket. Now and then
a picture looks as if it were washed with grey. On all the
pages, burnished gold was freely used. The Limbourgs were
talented artists and this manuscript is the most ornate example of their skill.

    A story is told of another manuscript in the Duc's
collection which had been purchased by the Rothschild family.
During the German occupation of France in World War II the
manuscript disappeared. Later, a soldier searching Goering's

house for stolen paintings found the manuscript in a waste basket. It was returned to the Rothschilds who gave it to the Bibliothèque Nationale in Paris.

Heures d'Anne de Bretagne

A few years ago friends of mine who were working on a "paper drive" found in a dark corner of a house a box of books. At the bottom of the box they discovered a large, heavy book of 238 pages, bound in brown imitation leather. The title page read: Heures d'Anne de Bretagne. It was a valuable facsimile of one of the most famous and most beautiful illuminated manuscripts. The original manuscript is in the Bibliothèque Nationale.

The Heures d'Anne de Bretagne was painted by Bourdichon about 1600 A.D. He was a teacher of artists, a designer of coins, lamps, banners and an illuminator of manuscripts. He made the wondrous manuscript for Anne, the Queen of King Charles VIII and later Queen of Louis XII. As was common to medieval Hour Books, Queen Anne herself was painted on the portrait pages.

The manuscript appears to have been done on ivory rather than on vellum. Gold plays around the figures. Costumes and jewelry glitter. The brief lines of script are carried to the margin with bands of brilliant color. It is in the wide borders that Bourdichon displays his imagination and his love of color. The borders are not massed with angel heads, elongated animals or geometric lines, but with flowers, fruits and vegetables. There are snails; a dragonfly with transparent wings lighting on a peach; an onion; and flowers in bud and blossom. So real are these illuminations that one is tempted to pick a rose or gather the vegetables.

The manuscript was bound in shagreen, a rude leather from the hides of horses, camels or asses. Great silver clasps adorned the binding.

As the Middle Ages came to a close the art of illumination reflected clearly the tremendous development in the art of the painter. This change can be easily demonstrated by a comparison of two portraits of the Virgin, one in the early Celtic Book of Kells, the other in the Heures d'Anne de Bretagne. The early painting depicts the Virgin with fingerless hands; turned out feet; almond shaped eyes under a high-

arched brow; a flat face circled with a profusion of yellow
hair. The painting in the Heures d'Anne de Bretagne is mas-
terful in color and grace. A gentle and exquisite Virgin in
flowing blue robes bends to teach the child, Jesus.

The Grimani Breviary

Illuminated a century before the Heures d'Anne de
Bretagne, the Grimani Breviary is a great, bulky codex of
832 leaves which required ten years for the completion of
the illumination. There is doubt as to the artist who painted
it, but it was probably done by many masters. At that time
artists were traveling from France to Italy and to the Low
Countries, stopping here and there to illuminate a few pages
or an entire book.

The Breviary was sold to Cardinal Grimani whose
name it bears. At the Cardinal's death it was given to his
nephew with the condition that it become the property of the
Republic of Venice. In the turmoil of Venetian wars, the
Breviary was taken to Rome where it disappeared. Upon re-
covery it was returned to Venice. One hundred and eighty
years ago the Breviary was finally placed in the safekeeping
of the Library of San Marco, Venice. In 1902, a corner of
the Library was damaged and anxious scholars inquired not
whether lives were lost but whether the Grimani Breviary was
safe. It was unharmed.

The marvelously beautiful manuscript contains the services and prayers recited by the priest. All the glory of
color, of perfect execution is there--the page borders heavy
with flowers, fruits and animals; the calendar pages with
scenes of medieval daily life; the landscapes; the splendid
pictures of Biblical events.

The binding of the Grimani Breviary is crimson velvet with the Grimani coat of arms in silver.

To select but six illuminated manuscripts for brief
descriptions is rather like setting a delicate gourmet dish
before a hungry man and not allowing him to eat.

It is most tempting to snatch a bite from the fare of
other famous manuscripts: to open the crimson velvet covers
of Queen Mary's Psalter and search for the Jesse tree, a
genealogy of the house of David; to appreciate the full meaning

of "Incp" in the great Bible of Alcuin; to smile at the crude
conception of the artist who in the Golden Gospels of St.
Medard simply put King Solomon's head on backward as the
mighty King, sword in one hand and the baby in the other,
turned to face the real mother; to enjoy the huge choir books
with a staff of four lines and stemless square notes--the music of the Mass; to wonder at the massive borders filled with
vases, urns, busts and statues in the Sforza Book of Hours.
These are but a small portion of the feast.

TRY THESE QUESTIONS

In reviewing this chapter, answer the following questions:

1. In column 1 are listed six famous manuscripts. In column 2 are listed libraries and museums which house these
manuscripts, numbered 1, 2, 3, 4, 5, 6, 7. Place in the
box in front of the manuscript, the correct number for the
library or museum which houses each manuscript.

Column 1	Column 2
☐ Grimani Breviary	1 Library of Congress
☐ The Book of Kells	2 British Museum
☐ Heures d'Anne de Bre- tagne	3 Trinity College, Dublin
	4 Pierpont Morgan Library
☐ The Lindisfarne Gospels	5 San Marco, Venice
☐ The Cottonian Genesis	6 New York Public Library
☐ Les Très Riches Heures	7 Bibliothèque Nationale, Paris

2. Illuminated manuscripts were often named after: 1) royalty; 2) a collector; or 3) the monastery where the manuscript
was copied. From which of the three sources were these
manuscripts named?

Example: 1   Queen Mary's Psalter (royalty)

☐ Cottonian Genesis

☐ Book of Kells

▱ Très Riches Heures du Duc de Berry

▱ The Lindisfarne Gospels

▱ Book of Durrow

3. Why do thousands of travelers visit Iona in the British Isles? _____

_____

4. Identify these terms as they apply to manuscripts:
    1. Bestiaries _____
    2. Books of Hours _____
    3. A Psalter _____
    4. An Antiphonary _____
    5. Septuagint _____
    6. X̄PI page _____

5. Why do scholars who specialize in a study of the Medieval Age treasure the calendar pages in the Book of Hours?

_____

_____

6. How does an historiated initial differ from a plain initial?

_____

_____

7. The illuminated manuscript flourished from the 6th century to the 15th century. What event caused the manuscript to be replaced? _____

8. The Celtic School of illumination had very pronounced characteristics which made it easy to identify. List below 3 of these characteristics.

    1 _____

    2 _____

    3 _____

9. Some illuminated manuscripts had borders filled with miniatures. What is a miniature? _____

_____

10.   What is the derivation of the word miniature?   _____

_____

        At this point, providing you have answered these ques-
tions correctly, you have made your own summary of this
chapter on illuminated manuscripts.

THINGS TO DO

1.   When you are next faced with the selection of a subject
for a brief paper in a social studies or literature course,
consider a study of one or two famous manuscripts not mentioned in this chapter.   You might begin your research by
consulting books noted in suggested readings at the end of
the chapter.

2.   With the help of your art teacher, design and illuminate
several capital letters.   You will find examples in the books
listed under further readings.   These letters make most at-
tractive Xmas cards.

3.   If you are planning a trip to New York City, why not include a visit to the Pierpont Morgan Library.   The most
beautiful illuminated manuscripts in the United States are
housed in this library.

4.   Check catalogs of filmstrips and slides for material on
illuminated manuscripts.   You may find them useful in giving
an oral report in an art or history class.

5.   You and a group of interested students might like to plan
a display on illuminated manuscripts for the library or for
corridor exhibit cases.   Gather material from such sources
as:
        Picture files in school and public libraries;
        Facsimiles of pages of manuscripts in postcard size may
            be purchased from museums and special libraries;
        Reproductions of manuscripts in museums and libraries
            in Europe might be brought to you by friends travel-
            ing abroad.

6.   Ask your librarian or teacher to write to the Pierpont
Morgan Library or the British Museum for illustrated book-
lets containing material on illuminated manuscripts.

7. Bookstores, private collectors and public libraries may
loan you facsimiles of manuscripts. Perhaps you have a
facsimile or two in your own book collection.

Do not consider the study of medieval manuscripts as
an interest only of the specialist in the book arts. For you
a study of manuscripts (hand-produced books) will illumine a
period in medieval history, art and literature, giving you new
understanding of the life of the people, the records they kept
and the manner in which they kept them.

FURTHER READING

Diringer, David. The Illuminated Book, Its History and Pro-
    duction. New York: Philosophical Library, 1958.
       Pictures and text combine to give rich and varied
facts about the illuminated manuscript. Readable and not too
technical. More than a textbook, as the author endows you
with his interest and delight in the illuminated manuscript.

Facsimiles. A facsimile is an exact copy. Begin your collection by asking a traveling friend to bring you postcard
facsimiles of manuscripts in libraries and museums. Visit
your public library and enjoy their facsimiles. Check with
your book store for inexpensive copies. Listed below are
two costly facsimiles of illuminated manuscripts and two low-
priced ones.

Henry, Françoise. The Book of Kells; Reproductions from
    the Manuscript in Trinity College, Dublin. New York:
    Knopf, 1974.
       Almost like sitting down with the original and thumb-
ing through it. A gorgeous book.

New York. Metropolitan Museum of Art. The Cloisters.
    The Belle Heures of Jean, Duke of Berry, Prince of
    France. New York: Metropolitan Museum of Art, 1958.
       A companion to the Très Riches Heures mentioned
in this chapter. Magnificent color, well produced.

New York. United Nations Educational, Scientific and Cul-
    tural Organization. Irish Illuminated Manuscripts of the
    Early Christian Period. New York: New American Li-
    brary, 1965.

France, Musée Condé à Chantilly.   <u>Les Très Riches Heures</u>
    <u>du Duc de Berry. Le Calendrier.</u> Paris: Nomis, n. d.
        This and the previous (UNESCO) item are well done
but inexpensive.

Rothe, Edith.   <u>Medieval Book Illumination in Europe.</u>   New
    York: W. M. Norton and Company, Inc. , 1966.
        "What's the good of a book without pictures?" asks
Alice in Wonderland.   A handsome book in color.   Enjoy it.

Chapter 6

LIBRARIES IN MEDIEVAL DAYS

"I have, God knows, an ample
field to plow and feeble oxen. "
--Chaucer

You may well wonder as you read of wars and pillage,
despotic rulers, feudalism and religious conflict, if there
could have been in medieval days either a time or a place
for quiet study and reflection. However, through this tapestry
of medieval life ran the bright thread of books and libraries
in the monasteries and universities.

Recognizing that books and libraries reflect the culture of the times, to understand medieval libraries one must
first review the tide of events known as the Medieval Age.

THE MEDIEVAL SCENE

The most miserable and turbulent years Europe ever
experienced are known to historians as the lower Middle
Age--the 6th to the 10th centuries. There were but two
years of peace, 749-751 A.D. "Woe to us," lamented Greg-
ory of Tours.

The Middle Ages began with the barbaric invasions.
Germanic tribes fled to Rome to escape the pillaging of the
Vandals. Led by their tribal chieftains, they paid small attention to art or literature, worshipped nature gods and hunted and fished for a livelihood. Chaos reigned in Rome.

Constantinople and the Eastern Empire

When Constantine turned toward the East to found Constantinople, the Roman Empire was divided. Classical culture moved into Europe on a Latin base and into the Eastern
Empire on a Greek base.

In 452 A.D. a university was established in Constantinople, and letters, science and all learning were treasured
and preserved by scholars. From the 7th to the 10th centuries, Constantinople became a new Rome. Churches, palaces, baths, forums, columns, statues, theatres, hospitals
and monasteries were magnificent--never equaled in the ancient world. A monetary system, engines of war, a fleet,
and a well-organized government under law marked an era
of extraordinary culture.

Art and architecture which appeared to have sunk under the waves of Teutonic invaders were nurtured by the By-
zantines. Illuminated manuscripts were superior in workmanship to those copied in European monasteries. Although several European schools of illumination, notably the Carolingian,
borrowed ideas freely, they did not attain the glory of Byzantine illumination until the 14th century.

Charlemagne and Alcuin

A bright light, too soon extinguished in the stormy
European world, was the reign of the Frankish King, Charlemagne, a hero of legend and romance. He set upon his
enemies in the name of God; dispensed justice; kept his
nobles loyal; built roads; opened trade routes and governed
wisely a large kingdom.

The most significant of his acts was to call to the
Royal Court the English scholar, Alcuin, who organized palace schools for the sons of nobles in preparation for careers
in the Church and at Court.

Alcuin's greatest task, however, was to direct the
copying of manuscripts. He taught the monastic scribes to
use a new handwriting called the Carolingian minuscule, a
mixture of capital and lower case (small) letters. By employing, for the first time, punctuation and paragraphing, the
readability of the Latin manuscripts, especially the text books,
was greatly improved. Try to copy a page in your chem-

istry text book using only capital letters, no punctuation
and employing many abbreviations. You will realize how difficult it must have been for a schoolboy to study his Latin
grammar.

Alcuin copied church literature in a beautiful Irish
uncial (rounded capitals) hand. Treasured by the British
Museum is Alcuin's great Bible.

Although Alcuin could not teach Charlemagne to write,
he so stimulated reading and copying in the monasteries that
it eventually spilled over into the monasteries of Fulda, Cor-
bie and St. Gall--centers of traditional learning in the Medieval Age.

Feudalism

During the 8th, 9th and 10th centuries, organized
government disintegrated and a way of life known as feudalism evolved. The knight on horseback became a symbol and
a ritual, his world ruled by a pledge of service to his King,
to his lord and to the defense of "maidens fair. " He hunted,
danced, jousted and listened as troubadours sang songs of
great deeds. Bravely, he defended his master, even unto
death. Vassals and serfs lived a life partly slave and partly
free. But the knight with a plumed helmet, his horse gaily
bedecked, was the "Batman" of medieval days.

Under feudalism life changed slowly. Due to poor
communication only a few of the people realized that great
cathedrals were being built, that towns were growing, trade
flourishing and nations struggling to be born. The people,
however, were acutely aware of the far-reaching power of
the Church in everyday life.

The Age of Faith

The Medieval Age has been called the Age of Faith.
God was worshipped in churches with the Mass and sacra-
ments, by king and serf alike. So great was the strength
of the Church that Holy Wars were waged in its name
against the Moslems. The five major attempts to capture
the Holy Sepulcher were known as the Crusades. Although
the Crusaders won no victories, their contact with the glory
of Byzantine and Moslem culture was of infinite value in the
enlightenment of Europe.

Yet another affirmation of faith appeared in the 13th
century with the rise of two quite diverse monastic orders,
the Dominicans and Franciscans, the latter known as the
friars or "begging missionaries." The Dominicans flocked
to the universities in order to become better preachers and
teachers. The Franciscans, true to their vow of poverty,
were organized by St. Francis of Assisi. The son of wealthy
parents, he carried to the darkest corners of the earth the
message of God's love for all creatures. To king and to
peasant he gave the quiet conviction that "God was in His
heaven."

The labors of these two monastic orders affected
greatly the basic doctrines of the medieval church.

Monastic Schools and Universities

Oriented to the Christian faith were the monastic and
the cathedral schools. Gaining some importance in the 13th
century, the cathedral school gradually merged into the university.

The monastic schools were of two types: an Inner
School for the training of the monks and an Outer School for
boys who were taught Latin and the Bible. The copying and
collecting of textbooks and religious manuscripts were an essential part of monastic education.

The Universities Rise. It was to the universities that
Europe owed its intellectual activity. In the 11th century,
Italy granted to Bologna the first university charter. A university at Paris developed from the Cathedral School of
Notre Dame. Oxford University in England received its charter early in the 1400s. Its library, originating in a corner
of St. Mary's Church, is today counted among the world's
great university libraries.

Life in the early universities was rough and tough.
Students, rich and poor, came in hordes. They "ran" the
university; hired the teachers and "fired" them if their lectures were dull or too long.

Many of the procedures in the early university have
continued to the present: the division of the university into
colleges; degrees such as B. A. , M. A. , Ph. D. ; the gown and
mortarboard; instruction by lectures and examinations.

The curriculum consisted of the seven Liberal Arts:
Grammar, Rhetoric, Logic, Astronomy, Mathematics, Geometry and Music. Mathematics was considered the most useless discipline. One could easily learn to count on an aba-
cus. Music was a most challenging discipline as melodies
could now be written with square stemless notes on a four-
line staff.

The Awakening. Scholars now questioned prevailing
ideas. At the University of Paris, Abelard, a vain but
brilliant scholar, disagreed with all accepted ideas. Thomas
Aquinas' belief that faith and reason could exist together was
denied by Duns Scotus, a Scottish philosopher.

Literary activity quickened. The great epics were recorded. Beowulf fought monsters in the dark fens of Britain.
The Cid died in mortal combat, strapped in his saddle. The
horn of Roland echoed over the valleys of France and the
Valkyrie snatched the dead in battle, carrying them in triumph to Valhalla. Dante wrote of Hell and Chaucer of a
band of pilgrims walking the dusty road to Canterbury. Religious mystery plays, poems and songs relieved the hum-
drum of every day life.

By 1500 A. D. the Medieval Age was reaping the glory
of the Renaissance. Nations had developed largely out of
disputes between the Crown and the Church. Spain had
closed its greatest history. France was living under powerful kings who believed that they were the State. England,
plagued by kings--good, bad and insane--had nevertheless
established a Parliament and had questioned the power of the
Pope.

Europe had schools, universities, art, literature, science, trade, government under nations--and books and libraries.

BOOKS AND LIBRARIES IN MEDIEVAL TIMES

In the monasteries, churches, cathedrals, colleges and
universities, books and manuscripts were gathered in small
collections. An early medieval library was considered most
fortunate if its collection numbered 500 manuscripts.

It is difficult to separate in time these various types

of libraries.   The monastic library didn't die on Monday.
The cathedral library wasn't born on Tuesday.   Each may
have had its "finest hour" but they overlapped and comple-
mented each other, one type of library merging into another
as did the cathedral library into the university library.

The Monastic Book Room

How the monastic library changed its monastic face
into a university one is a brief story.

The monastery of Bobbio in Italy probably housed in
its Book Room the largest monastic collection--666 books
and manuscripts.   How do we know the number?   The library
catalog written on vellum is preserved in the Vatican Library.
Another large collection was housed in the monastery at Fulda, Germany.   Several of the precious monastic manuscripts
have been preserved at Fulda.   Small but important monastic
collections were assembled in the English monasteries of St.
Albans, Canterbury, Durham and Winchester.

It is well to remember that monastic libraries began
in the scriptorium at Monte Cassino, Italy.   Under the Rule
of St. Benedict the monks copied, read, studied and preserved manuscripts.   But there came a day when the collections outgrew the scriptorium and a separate library room
was built over the cloisters as a part of the chapter house.
This book room was long and narrow, measuring 80' x 15',
with equidistant windows over the cloister arches.   It is in-
structive to compare the meager 500 pounds spent to build a
library room in the monastery of St. Albans with the eight
million dollars spent to build a modern rural school without
a library.

A long, stone staircase led to the entrance of the library.   The floors were wooden, and the stark interior was
relieved by a decorated ceiling and carved wainscoting.   Book
presses were placed against the wall opposite the windows.
The coarsely-made, heavy, two-doored presses were replaced
later with presses of polished woods, carved with intricate
designs.

Within the press, each shelf (gradus) was numbered
from the bottom up: I, II, III.   The presses were lettered
A, B, C.   The first book on the shelf was numbered 1.   In
short, C II 4 might be dubbed a monastic library call number.

History, Geography, Sermons, Grammar and Divinity were
the subject headings under which the contents of the presses
were organized. A catalog of the holdings listed all but the
precious books. These titles were withheld for fear of
thieves.

More and more books were demanded by the universities. To house these collections more space was required
and, with the subsequent expansion, more attention was given
to the attractiveness of the library room.

Windows were decorated with iron scrollwork and coats
of arms in painted glass. Ceilings were vaulted, arched,
rounded, frescoed or elaborately carved. Then appeared the
book stack, eight feet tall, made of mahogany inlaid with
cedar and ebony, divided by fluted wooden columns and mounted on a handsome, carved base. Moreover, the shelving
was placed in an alcove arrangement jutting out from the
wall between equidistant windows, often with a long lectern
or reading desk between each stack.

How did the massive book presses change into tall,
graceful book stacks? An English scholar, John Clark, *
has filled a fat volume on the changing form of the medieval
library. These changes are paraphrased in the following
steps.

A Lectern Changes into a Book Stack

Step 1. The Zutphen Lecturn. This slanted reading
desk upon which a manuscript or a book might be spread,
was named after a church in Zutphen, Holland, where it was
first used as furniture in a library.

The lectern was long, with a bench pulled up in front
of it. Running along the top of the lectern was a metal rod,
locked with elaborate hardware into the uprights at each end
of the lectern. On the rods slid iron rings. Attached to
the rings were chains 12" long, made of hammered iron links
ending with a swivel. The swivel was attached to an iron
plate fastened to the front of the book. Thus the book was
chained to the lectern.

*John W. Clark, The Care of Books. (Cambridge: Cam-
bridge University Press, 1901).

Even later, when book stacks were used, the books were chained to the shelves. A chained library, dated 1412, may be seen in restoration at Hereford Cathedral, England. Also preserved in the Cathedral are two 14th century book presses.

It was necessary to medieval days to chain books. Why? Books were costly, in great demand, and there were robbers.

Step 2. The Double Lectern. A slanting desk was now placed on the opposite side of the original lectern. The two lecterns, back to back, were secured to decorated end pieces which were mounted on a decorated base. Hardward on the end pieces locked in the rod across the top of the double lectern upon which rings and chains secured the books on both lecterns. A bench was placed on each side of the lectern.

A mini-diagram of the end elevation of a lecture may be of help.

top, often pointed and carved

hardware to lock in rods

lecterns

Step 3. The Michelangelo Lectern. A beautiful lectern was designed by the great artist for the Laurentian Library (Biblioteca Laurenziana) in Florence, Italy. As you read further in this chapter you will find a description of these unusual lecterns in the story of the Laurenziana.

Step 4. The Lectern Adds Shelves. At first a shelf was added below the lectern, then above the lectern. Up and up climbed the shelves, and up and up climbed the end pieces. A book stack! For a time the slanted lectern was used as a place to rest a heavy volume. Sometimes a lectern was hinged so that it might be dropped down when not in use. Then the lectern gradually disappeared as a part of the book stack. Occasionally a low double lectern and benches were retained between the stacks for consulting heavy books. You may have used one in your school library when consulting encyclopedias and atlases.

As the shelves and end pieces of the stack mounted higher, the end pieces were often richly decorated. The wooden tops might be pointed, carved or ornamented with wooden urns. On a strip of vellum, nailed to the end of the stack, was a list, by author and title, of the books standing on that particular stack.

Step 5. Alcove or Stall Shelving. From book presses standing against the wall to tall book stacks jutting out into the room between equidistant windows came a major change in the slow process of library arrangement. An increase in the numbers of both books and readers demanded a better use of space. Rather startling combinations of wall and stall shelving led to unusual library interiors. For example, in Sir Christopher Wren's restoration of Lincoln (England) Cathedral Library, the alcoves formed by the stacks were closed off by beautifully ornamented doors. A quiet place for study was a necessary part of service in medieval libraries. Today, a sign bearing the word Silence signifies in the public's mind the austere presence of books.

Step 6. The Standing Lectern. This library arrangement was experimental and was used principally in university libraries. The standing lectern was so named because scholars were obliged to stand to consult books. A rail running across the bottom of the lectern was thoughtfully provided so that a scholar might rest one foot at a time. Above the waist-high lectern was a shelf with books chained to the rods. The slanted, wooden top of the lectern bore in large capital letters the name of the subject shelved on each particular lectern: Medici, Historic, Mathematic. The lecterns were placed in two rows the length of the library room with an aisle between the alcoves. The most famous example of the standing lectern, dated 1610, was at Leyden University in Holland.

It is difficult to imagine a modern day student standing for hours to consult research materials. The medieval student did not approve either, and the standing lectern was short-lived.

Step 7. Wall Shelving. Wall shelving was no innovation, but solid wall shelving from floor to ceiling was. To give access to the books either tall ladders or balconies were necessary. A balcony built around the room was preferred.

The first use of floor to ceiling wall shelving was in

the library room of the Escorial in Spain. The best known
use of this library arrangement was at the Bodleian, Oxford
University. The Selden and Arts Ends, opening off the Duke
Humphrey Library, were fitted with ceiling-high wall shelving.

While these seven steps may appear logical, remember
that a variety of arrangements might be employed even in one
library--lectern, alcove stacks and wall shelving. When you
walk into a modern university library, with free standing
stacks arranged according to use, picture a library of books
chained to lecterns.

It was a distinct privilege in medieval times for a
scholar to use a library. But use it he did, in spite of a
multitude of rules and regulations.

Rules and Regulations in a Medieval Library

To walk into a library at any time of day or night,
consult materials and borrow them freely is a very different
conception of library service than was faced by the medieval
borrower. In early days one manuscript was loaned to each
monk once a year, usually at the beginning of Lent. The loan
was accompanied by dire warnings about the care of the manuscript. For example, pages were to be turned only after the
sleeve of the monk's robe was pulled down to cover his dirty
hands. A curse was placed upon the head of whoever mu-
tilated or stole a manuscript.

In the early university, the library was open only
during daylight hours. Neither candles nor an open fire were
allowed; books were too precious. Library doors were secured at night by three locks, with keys held by three different officials of the university. Very valuable books and
all records were kept in chests, closed by three locks.

Restrictions were placed upon the borrowing of books.
Each book had a high value set upon it and punishment for
default was severe. The use of books might be withheld for
a year or an offender might lose his Fellowship.

At one college of Oxford University only a graduate
student with eight years of Philosophy was permitted to study
in the libraries and he had to promise to close his book
properly, close the windows, search the library for thieves,
and close and lock the door.

        At Magdalen College (Oxford) a book could not be
loaned outside of the College nor taken out of town in "whole
or in sheets," even by a Master. Students could not exchange borrowed books without the permission of at least
three Deans. If a book were loaned, it must be returned by
nightfall.

        A medieval student seldom owned a book. As more
books became available, he might rent one, page by page.
Denied to him was the pleasure, common among students today, of building his own collection.

Armarius, Prefect, Keeper of Books, Librarian

        When a candidate is interviewed today for a position
as librarian in a high school, three questions are usually
asked. What books have you read? Why do you enjoy working with young adults? What do you consider to be the most
important services a librarian can give?

        Sensible enough questions, but not the ones asked of
a prospective librarian in the Medieval Age. The first question might have been: Do you hold Holy Orders? Have you
studied Philosophy for at least eight years? Can you keep
accurate records? A positive answer to these questions was
essential if a librarian were to serve in an early university
library.

        From the days of the Alexandrian Library (326 B. C.)
it was required that the librarian first of all be a scholar.
In the English monasteries and universities, the librarian
must have completed eight years in Philosophy; hold Holy
Orders; say Mass daily; explain, in public lectures, difficult
Biblical passages. He must make a detailed catalog of the
books by author and title and keep a faithful record of all
borrowers. The name of the borrower and the title of the
book were written on large tablets covered with parchment
and wax. When the book was returned the entry was pressed
out.

        Once a year all books were "laid out," counted and
identified. If a book was missing, the librarian was forced
to pay for it.

        Perhaps the most difficult task required of the librar-
ian was to procure books. Donors were eagerly sought, and

the choice of books was limited by a strict censorship exercised by the university.

The librarian was responsible for "keeping order" in the room and he must constantly be on guard against fire and theft, the most common dangers to books. As a reward for all these tasks, he was given four yards of woolen cloth for a gown and hood.

THE MEDIEVAL BOOK SELLERS

No book publishers. No book clubs. No paperbacks. No rental libraries. No book stores.

By the 13th century, book sellers gathered around the universities, especially the famous ones at Padua, Paris, Bologna and Oxford. Textbooks were copied by scribes and sometimes rented page by page ("in sheets" is the proper term) to students. If you were a wealthy student and could afford to buy an entire text, you patiently waited while an army of scribes copied it for you. Books were expensive, indeed. In France, a quantity of wheat might be exchanged for a page of a book. The more fortunate student hired a servant to carry about his heavy books. Furthermore, he was forced to pay for space in a library in order to lay down his books.

The universities kept a close watch on the booksellers. Only certain translations of a text could be copied and these must be most accurate. Fines for infringement of this regulation were imposed.

The booksellers were called stationarii, hence our words stationer (one who has a station for the sale of books and writing materials) or stationery (pens, ink and paper).

The invention of printing was about to make a terrific impact on the availability of books and on the tradition surrounding booksellers.

THE PHILOBIBLION: A FIRST BOOK ON
BOOK COLLECTING IN MEDIEVAL TIMES

In the library of his palace, the Duke of Urbino gathered a magnificent collection. Several generations of the Medici family assembled precious manuscripts and books for their libraries. Kings and their mistresses delighted in lavish gifts of manuscripts. Duke Humphrey, a versatile collector, gave his books to Oxford University.

However, the most notorious of the medieval book collectors was Richard de Bury, Bishop of Durham, tutor to King Edward III of England, Dean of Wells Cathedral, Treasurer Royal, Lord Privy Seal and Ambassador to Rome. De Bury made good use of his offices, honestly or otherwise, to add to his collection.

De Bury appeared to glory in the ownership of books. He filled every corner of his house and was obliged to jump over piles of books to reach his bed. What became of his books is not known. De Bury died without possessions. His servants stole his household goods and all of his clothes except for the undershirt in which he died.

As a book collector de Bury captivated booksellers and persuaded monks to open old presses where the manuscripts were covered with mice litter and raddled with worms. He surrounded himself with a multitude of scribes, binders and illuminators. Those manuscripts and books he could not possess, he had the scribes copy.

De Bury was the author of a famous book, Philobiblion, an essay on the art of book collecting. His notes on the care of books are amusing. He begs the reader to treat a book more carefully than he treats his boots; to open and close a book properly; to be sure his hands are clean; to wipe his nose often so as not to bedew the book; to avoid reading while eating or talking, as sputtering from a full mouth might shower the book; to refrain from scratching the itch and pimples while reading; to mark the place in the book with a straw lest the binding be broken; to put the book gently aside rather than throwing it across the room when bitten by a flea. If you read between the lines bits and pieces of the social life of medieval days are revealed.

By their gifts of books and manuscripts, the famous medieval collectors, the Medici and Duke Humphrey, laid the

foundation stones of two notable libraries which are still extant: the Laurenziana in Florence, Italy, designed by Michelangelo, and the Bodleian at Oxford University, considered by
many scholars to be the most distinguished university library
in the world.

THE LAURENZIANA

With roots deep in medieval times, the Laurenziana
and the Bodleian University Library challenge the imagination
and are deserving of at least an armchair journey.

The Library of the Medici

Consider yourself standing in Florence, Italy. The
horrible mud floods a few years ago took their toll, but the
numbers of people, especially college students, who hastened
to Florence to help in the "clean-up" was clear evidence of
the reverence with which the magnificent Florentine art was
regarded.

In Florence, close to the Church of San Lorenzo where
Savonarola thundered out his defiance, and in which Michelangelo is entombed, is the Laurenziana (Laurentian) Library
founded by the Medici.

Cosimo de Medici began the famed collection of manuscripts in 1389 with three titles: the Gospels, a book of
Sermons and the Legend of St. Margaret. He surrounded
himself with 45 scribes and later boasted of 63 titles in his
collection. Cosimo traveled across Europe and the East in
search of manuscripts, always carrying with him his own
precious manuscripts wrapped in oilskin and towels. In 1444,
he built a library at San Marco and with a grand gesture
opened it to the public. The Florentines may well have regarded this privilege as a sop to the harshness of life under
the Medicis.

Cosimo's son, Piero, continued to add to the collection glorious illuminated manuscripts and miniatures in frames
of gold and jewels. He adopted a unique arrangement for his
library, using the color of the binding to identify the books:
blue for Theology, purple for Poetry and yellow for Grammar.

The collection then passed to Piero's son, Lorenzo, known as Lorenzo the Magnificent, who was a poet rather than a collector. He kept many of the wondrous manuscripts about him at his villa--manuscripts on medicine, laws, drama, history, poetry, orations, Books of Hours, the Gospels, the writings of Dante, Petrarch, Aristotle, Euripides and other Greek dramatists. Lorenzo was generous with the manuscripts; one was loaned to a scholar for 35 years.

In the year that Columbus found a new world, Lorenzo died. Two years later the Medici were driven out of Florence, their palace destroyed and their manuscripts scattered, a few of them taken to Rome for safe-keeping.

Then in 1571, under the guidance of Pope Clement, the Laurenziana, named for Lorenzo the Magnificent, was built over the cloisters of the Church of San Lorenzo. Three thousand of the priceless manuscripts were reassembled and placed in the Laurenziana, a monument to the Medici family.

A Great Artist at Work

Designed by Michelangelo the Laurenziana "stands alone in beauty." The exterior of the library was never finished. Stone niches are empty of their intended statuary. A most graceful staircase into the library was built on the form of a barrel, and it "floats."

The interior library room is long and narrow. Fifteen equidistant windows bear in color the Medici coat of arms. The ceiling is flat and wondrously carved. The red pavement of the wide center aisle is boldly designed in yellow with devices of the Medici family.

Most unusual are the lecterns and benches, made of walnut and placed in two rows the length of the room. The high back of a bench forms the support for the lectern on the other side, thus producing a graceful, uninterrupted flow of line. Rods, secured by locks at the end of each lectern-bench, run below the lectern. The book chains, designed by Michelangelo and considered the most beautiful ever made, are of iron, 2'3" long and 1/8" wide, the links flattened at the end.

Manuscripts were spread open on the lecterns and remained so for nearly 400 years. In 1920 it became necessary to move them out of sight, the chains still attached.

The number of manuscripts and incunabula grew slowly, but each item added was a rare one.   As late as 1920,
a most distinguished prefect (librarian) awakened scholars to
a realization of the rich content of this library.

THE BODLEIAN, OXFORD UNIVERSITY

At this point change from your "traveling armchair"
labeled The Laurenziana to one with The Bodleian written
across the back.

St. Mary's Church.   The Duke Humphrey Library.
The Selden and Arts Ends.   The Radcliffe Camera.   These
words spell the history of a remarkable university library--
the Bodleian at Oxford, England.

In the 13th century, in a small room in St. Mary's
Church, the birthing room of the Bodleian, were housed in
presses and in chains a few manuscripts.   When a library
room was built in 1410, the manuscripts must indeed have
rattled their chains in an almost empty room.

The Duke Humphrey Library

Unhappy at the scarcity of manuscripts deemed proper
for a university library, Humphrey, Duke of Gloucester and
uncle of Henry VI of England, made gifts to the library from
his private collection.   The Duke lived like the Prince he
was.   His favorite occupation was collecting books and manuscripts, and he pursued it in scholarly fashion, buying and
exchanging in the book markets of France, Germany and Italy.
In his lifetime he gave the university some 600 manuscripts
and books.

Space for these gifts was extended to a second floor
and, in 1488, this innermost shrine of the future Bodleian
library was opened and named the Duke Humphrey Library in
honor of its generous donor.

When King Henry VIII ordered the confiscation of manuscripts and books that in any way savored of the Papacy,
many of Duke Humphrey's books were destroyed.   The few
that were left are now preserved in the British Museum, London.   The library was neglected, desks were broken and manu-

scripts sold for the vellum on which they were copied. Oxford University had no library.

Sir Thomas Bodley

Then in 1598 came Sir Thomas Bodley, diplomat,
traveler, collector and later a Knight of the Realm. So
vigorous were his efforts in behalf of the restoration of a
library at Oxford that at its dedication the library was named
in his honor.

Within six years, Bodley had gathered 6,000 volumes,
many of them gifts. It became the fashion to donate books to
Bodley's library. Bodley kept a strict watch on the contents
of the gifts and purchases; he preferred Protestant theology
and discarded Shakespeare as "riffle raffle." A printed catalog was published, perhaps the first of its kind in a university
library.

Bodley was equally strict in his orders to his first
librarian, Thomas James. Marriage was forbidden, and
James subsequently resigned. Bodley accepted his resigna-
tion promptly, claiming that James was a slow cataloger and
that his handwriting was impossible.

The library room was also restored, with decorated
windows and a ceiling painted with the coat-of-arms of both
Bodley and the university. Stacks replaced the lecterns.
So rapidly did the collection grow that in 1610 the Arts End
was added and fitted with the first ceiling-high wall shelving
to be used in England.

Shortly after Bodley died in 1613, the Selden End was
added. The floor plan of Oxford University library now re-
sembled the letter H, the restored Duke Humphrey library as
the cross bar and the Arts and Selden Ends as the uprights.

There was alarm over the crowding of the shelves,
and Sir Christopher Wren, the notable architect, was called
in to prevent the collapse of the building. A third floor was
added but it was used largely as a museum in which were
displayed such items as a coat worn by the Tsar of Russia,
a stuffed crocodile and the dried body of a boy.

The years from 1780-1860 brought tremendous additions of illuminated manuscripts, incunabula, first editions

and a copy of every book published in England. The Radcliffe Camera (a round tower) was built to hold the overflow
resulting from the vast influx of materials.

Today, four million books, 40,000 manuscripts, and
18,000 charters, deeds and rolls embodying the tradition of
England are housed in the Bodleian at Oxford University.

The Bodleian and Laurenziana had their roots in medieval times. Among other distinguished collections that made
books and libraries a tremendous force in medieval culture
were the Vatican Library and the magnificent royal library of
King Matthias Corvinus of Hungary.

As the medieval period came to a close, the monastic
manuscripts and the separate monastic library building were
of incalculable value in the rebirth of the library after the
Dark Ages. Whether for the monastic schools, for the scholar who revered the classics, or for the creation of a "thing
of beauty," manuscripts were copied, illuminated and preserved to the Glory of God.

The university fostered books and libraries and inspired the quest of man in an understanding of other men in
an awakening world.

The 14th and 15th centuries brought a bright and vigorous period known as the Renaissance. In the new learning
based on the ancient authors and stimulated by Petrarch and
other humanistic scholars, man became aware that he was an
individual with a chance to live a life of his own.

He witnessed explorers sailing the oceans, printers
pulling down the handles of their printing presses, towns extending horizons, exchanges in trade, nations gaining an identity and religious thought offering a measure of freedom.

The monastic, university and private libraries in medieval times--their traditions, buildings, collections and organ-
ization--were remarkable forerunners of the great modern
library.

A BOOK REPORT: "GREAT LIBRARIES"

No, this is not an assignment for a book report. It is a request to give your attention to a book which will bring the color and majesty of medieval manuscripts, books and libraries alive before your eyes.

Ask your librarian to obtain this special book for you or request a copy as a gift for your personal book collection.

The author of the book is Anthony Hobson and the title is Great Libraries,* printed in England and published in New York in 1970.   Each page of the book records, in pictures, a story in the life of the book.

As you enjoy Great Libraries, recognize landmarks with which you are already acquainted--the great B (Beatus) in a manuscript copied in 872 A.D. at the monastery at St. Gall; a monk at his lectern, copying a manuscript; the Bodleian and the cloisters of San Lorenzo with the walls of the Laurenziana rising behind it; a sumptuous university library room at Coimbra, built by King John V of Portugal; the library at Trinity College, Dublin where the treasured Book of Kells is displayed; the artist's sketch of the proposed new British Museum, or the magnificence of the Salone Sistono in the Vatican.

Who knows? You may one day be moved in your enthusiasm to write a book report on Great Libraries.

FURTHER READING

Hobson, Anthony. Great Libraries. New York: G. P. Putnam's Sons, © 1970.
    A treasure house of information on 32 famous libraries--cathedral, university, monastic, private and national. The photographs are magnificent in detail and well produced. A return again and again to this fascinating book is guaranteed.

*Anthony Hobson, Great Libraries. (New York, G. P. Putnam's Sons, © 1970).

National Geographic Society. <u>Age of Chivalry.</u> Washington:
National Geographic Society, © 1969.
Recommended for your pleasure. One of the beauti-
ful volumes in the <u>Story of Mankind Library</u> issued by the
National Geographic Society. The medieval age lives in pictures galore, in color and in black and white. Add this book
to your personal library.

Streeter, Burnett H. <u>The Chained Library: A Survey of
Four Centuries in the Evolution of the English Library.</u>
London: Macmillan, 1931.
With infinite care an old chained library has been
restored at Hereford Cathedral in England. A good initiation
to the patient work of a scholar. Illustrated.

Thompson, James Westfall. <u>The Medieval Library.</u> New
York: Hafner, 1957.
A famous historian writes in detail about medieval
libraries. Perhaps "too much of a muchness" for you, but
read Chapter 1 carefully.

Chapter 7

CHINA AND GUTENBERG GIVE
PRINTING TO THE WORLD

"If the first Prometheus brought fire
from heaven in a fennel-stalk, the last
will take it back in a book. "
                    --John Cowper Powys

As teletypes and satellites pour out the news from a-
round the world and giant computerized printing presses pour
it back to the world, there stands in the distant shadows of
the past a Chinese wood carver, bent over a block of wood
into which he had cut a Chinese character.

Thus begins in China the miracle of print.

PRINTING IN CHINA

Six centuries before Johann Gutenberg invented printing by movable type, the Chinese were printing by means of
wood blocks--a process called xylography.

One day a wood carver took a block of soft pear wood,
a sharp knife and cut a few Chinese characters in relief;
that is, the picture of the characters stood out from the
wooden block. Then he inked the picture and pressed thin,
Chinese-made paper down on the inked surface. He printed.

Meantime in a monastic writing room a monk was
bent over a lectern, with tired fingers copying a Bible, using
a quill pen and parchment.

Since the Chinese and Japanese worshipped the god,

108

Buddha, the Empress Shotoku of Japan ordered in the year
770 A.D. that a million charms be printed by wood blocks.
These charms, pictures of Buddha, were printed on tightly
rolled strips of paper and placed in a tiny wicker cage.
Worshippers at a Buddhist shrine bought the charms to hang
above their home altars.   Several of these charms may be
seen today in the British Museum, London.

Sir Aurel Stein, an explorer and an archeologist,
came one day in his travels upon the Cave of the Thousand
Buddhas.   Here he found, behind a wall and perfectly preserved in the dry desert air, 1,130 bundles of printed papers,
known to scholars today as the Tun-Huang papers.

Among the rolls was the first dated printed book, the
Diamond Sutra, so named because it was given to Queen Victoria at the celebration of her diamond Jubilee.   The Diamond
Sutra, containing Buddhist scripture, consisted of seven sheets
of paper pasted together to form a roll 16 feet long and a foot
wide.   But the most amazing part of the roll was the colophon, which read: "Printed May 11, 868 A.D. by Wang
Chieh ... to honor his parents. " Thus the roll bore the
name of the printer and the date of the earliest extant printing of a book by means of wood blocks.   The work was so
magnificently done that the Chinese must have had much practice in this method of printing before the Diamond Sutra was
produced.   It is one of the treasures of the British Museum
--priceless, ageless.

By means of wood blocks the Chinese also printed
paper money and playing cards.   Dice and dominoes, probably the earliest games known to man, had been carved on
bone or ivory.   Now the faces of the dice were transferred
to paper and became dice sheets or playing cards.   It is a
long story from these flimsy, dotted pieces of Chinese paper
to today's brightly decorated decks of playing cards.   Many
studies have been made of the evolution of playing cards; it
is a fascinating subject with historic overtones.

PRINTING IN KOREA

Korea about 1100 A.D. enjoyed a renaissance in art
and learning.   It is not surprising that the idea of printing
by movable type rather than by wood blocks was attempted
in view of the demand for learning materials.   Pi Sheng made

characters out of clay, baked them and set them in resin
(wax) on an iron plate.   But when paper was pressed down
on the inked characters, they toppled.

        The Chinese scorned this Korean attempt.   With 3,000
characters in their "alphabet," a font of type was neither practical nor artistic.   They preferred printing by wood blocks.
By this method they produced a monumental encyclopedia of
6,000 volumes.

PRINTING MOVES WESTWARD

        At long last Europeans began to wonder at this "print-
ing" coming from China.   The Mongols brought wood block
prints with them as they crossed Persia, Russia and Germany
on their way to conquer the world.   The Crusaders learned
about printing from wood blocks as they moved toward the
capture of the Holy City.   Caravans crossed the trade routes
of Europe loaded with jewels, silks, spices and playing cards.
In fact, card playing became so popular that it was forbidden,
especially for the working classes.   Of course, the Church
frowned on any form of printing, preferring the monk, the
quill and the parchment rather than this pagan nonsense.

The Image Prints

        However, awakening intellectual curiosity in Europe
prevailed and image prints (Heiligen) were produced in the
Low Countries by the wood block method.   A picture and a
brief moral saying were cut in relief.   The face of the block
was inked.   Damp paper was laid on and rubbed with a cloth
pad stuffed with wool.

        The image prints were sacred in nature--a picture of
Jesus, the Virgin or a Saint.   Even as the Chinese carried
home a charm of Buddha, so the medieval Pilgrim visiting
a shrine purchased an image print and built a home altar
around it.

        Best known of early European image prints is the St.
Christopher.   A copy was found by chance inside the cover
of a wooden codex.   The print has been dated circa 1423
A. D.   On paper in brown ink is a picture of St. Christopher
carrying the Christ Child across a stream.   St. Christopher

holds a palm tree as a staff.   In the corners of the print are
a peasant driving a donkey, a miller carrying grain up a
path to his cottage, a Saint holding a lantern high to light St.
Christopher across the water.   Under the picture are two
lines in Latin.   Freely translated the lines read:

> Each day that thou the likeness of St. Christopher
> shalt see,
> That day no frightful form of death shall make an
> end of thee.

Reading this legend of St. Christopher you may now
understand why people often wear a St. Christopher medal
or fasten a small statue of St. Christopher onto the top of
the instrument panel of a car.

Block Books

The next step in printing was a logical one.   Instead
of a one-page image print, a series of pages were cut--an
entire story on wood blocks.   The pages were fastened together and a block book was born.   Many stories were thus
printed with pictures and a few words of text in Latin either
below the picture or on ribbons winding in and around the
picture.

Bible stories with a moral lesson were most popular
and the best selling block books were the Ars Moriendi and
the Biblia Pauperum.

The Ars Moriendi (The Art of Dying) was issued in
Latin, French and German.   The pictures were frightening.
Devils tempted the dying man and Angels pled for his im-
mortal soul.

Biblia Pauperum (Poor Man's Bible) was a picture
book consisting of a three-paneled page with a picture in
each panel.   The center picture depicted an incident from
the New Testament, the Devil tempting Christ.   The pictures
on either side were from the Old Testament and portrayed
the same moral lesson, "lead us not into temptation. "

Block books were inexpensive and so popular that they
were sold in large numbers even after books printed by
movable type were available.

JOHANN GUTENBERG AND THE INVENTION
OF PRINTING BY MOVABLE TYPE

Now Europe prepared to "wake up" and the demand for books grew. The materials for printing were at hand--paper, oil paints for making printer's ink, metals used by workers who knew their craft, and presses used for crushing grapes and olives. All things were favorable. But Europe needed a genius. Johann Gutenberg was there.

However, as printing by movable type began its first faltering steps, three questions need to be asked and answered. When was printing by movable type invented? Probably between 1440 and 1455. Where was printing by movable type invented? Possibly in Strasbourg or Mainz, Germany. Who invented printing by movable type? We do not know; it was probably Johann Gutenberg, although no piece of printing bears his name as a printer. In the great catalog of the British Museum listing early printers, the name of Johann Gutenberg does not appear.

Scholars agree and disagree, search records and search them again for firm evidence as to the inventor of printing by movable type. Gutenberg? Yes? No? Fust and Schoeffer? Yes? No? Laurens Janszoon Coster of Haarlem? Yes? No?

Unless and until scholars stumble onto some not yet discovered document, the evidence points to Gutenberg as the inventor of printing by movable type.

His Life and Contribution

Born Johann Gensfleisch, no document bears the date of his birth, though it was probably about 1400. He took his mother's name--Gutenberg. The family was banished from Mainz and went to live in Strasbourg. In 1438 young Gutenberg took two partners into his "business," making mirrors, coins and medals, or possibly designing type faces. On two different occasions Gutenberg borrowed money for a "secret" project. Silence. The family returned to Mainz and Gutenberg borrowed money from John Fust, a wealthy citizen of Mainz in order to "finish the work." We can only surmise that it was printing. Gutenberg could not repay the loan. Fust sued Gutenberg and Fust "got the tools." Shortly, Fust and his son-in-law, Peter Schoeffer, who had been Gutenberg's best workman, set up a printing shop.

And what of Johann Gutenberg? He may have continued to operate a small printing press, but not a piece of printed material carries his name. He died in 1468, his burial place unknown. In Mainz, a museum was opened in his honor with exhibits of his printing and with at least 50 portraits of him. Some scholars claim that very little in the museum is authentic.

The Gutenberg Imprints

A listing of Gutenberg imprints is presented here so that you may at some future time recognize a title or two and nod knowingly when the Constance Missal is mentioned as a treasure of the Pierpont Morgan Library in New York City. You should also be alert that some scholars make grave accusations as to the authenticity of certain imprints.

Fragment of the World Judgment: a scrap of paper bearing a part of a poem dealing with the Last Judgment. Discovered in 1892 and now in the Gutenberg Museum at Mainz, Germany.

A Donatus: a Latin grammar, the popular school book of the 1400s. A copy of the third issue is in the Bibliothèque Nationale in Paris.

An Astronomical Calendar: a faded page found in the binding of a book. Ascribed to the year 1448.

An Indulgence: issued by the Pope to further a cause he deemed worthy. Usually written by hand, hundreds of copies could now be quickly made by this new invention of printing. Copies of the 1454 Indulgence are preserved in the Bibliothèque Nationale in Paris and in the Pierpont Morgan Library in New York City.

The 42-line Bible: so called because 40-42 lines are printed on a page. A copy of this magnificent Bible with decorations in red and blue was bound and dated 1456 by the vicar of a church in Mainz. Although it is commonly known as the Gutenberg Bible, it was probably printed in 1455 by Fust and Schoeffer of Mainz, from the types Fust obtained when he sued Gutenberg for an unpaid loan. Thirty-two copies of the 42-line Bible are in existence today. The copies in the Yale University Library and in the Bibliothèque Nationale are considered to be the most perfect.

The 36-line Bible: the "true" Gutenberg Bible. Only
8 copies are in existence and are jealously guarded. This
Bible is not well printed. The type is large and awkward
and spaces have been left for initial letters in the manner of
the illuminated manuscripts. It was probably printed in 1450
from an experimental type face which Gutenberg did not give
to Fust at the time of the law suit.

One stands in wonder before the perfection of the 42-
line Bible. How could such a beautiful book be produced at
the very beginning of the art of printing? The 36-line Bible,
however, holds a unique place in printing history and testi-
fies to Gutenberg's persistence as a printer and as a man
who had a vision denied to him.

An amusing story is told of a lad who came one day
into the Pierpont Morgan Library in New York City. He
asked to see the Gutenberg Bible. A guard watched closely
as the lad counted the lines of print on a page. He then
announced in a loud voice, "This is not the Gutenberg Bible.
There are 42 lines on a page." It so happened that Belle da
Costa Greene, Mr. Morgan's distinguished librarian, over-
heard the lad's statement. As she questioned him, she found
that he had hoped to see the 36-line Bible. Miss Greene
allowed that if he were clever enough to know the difference
between the two Bibles, the Morgan copy of the 36-line Bible
should be brought to him. The lad examined it with care.
Now he had seen the Gutenberg Bible.

The Constance Missal: The Pierpont Morgan Library
possesses one of the four known copies, dated about 1450 and
believed to have been the earliest Gutenberg imprint. This
claim is challenged by many scholars.

A Catholican: the last known Gutenberg imprint, a
Latin dictionary dated 1460.

It is beside the point to belabor the mystery of the
man who first printed by means of movable type. Cutting
metal type faces for the Latin alphabet, perfecting an ink
that wouldn't smear under pressure, finding paper sturdy
enough to carry the ink, and a locking device that would
firmly hold the type in place on the bed of a press were
monumental tasks. That they were the work of Johann Gutenberg is at least probable.

A colophon in a book printed in 1468 by Peter Schoeffer states that printing was invented by two John's--John
Gutenberg and John Fust. Discovered in the library of the

Sorbonne, Paris, was this statement: "the act of printing was first of all invented by one John, whose surname was Gutenberg." Douglas McMurtrie, an authority on Gutenberg, states, "Printing was probably done between 1450 and 1454 in or near Mainz, probably by John Gutenberg."

CRADLE BOOKS

Before continuing this brief review of early printing, mention must be made of incunabula--"cradle books." By definition, books printed by movable type before January 1501 were called incunabula, the plural form of the Latin word incunabulum, meaning cradle.

Amazingly enough, these early printed books established the basic form of the book as it exists today--title page, illustration, pagination, punctuation, and printer's marks.

What was the nature of these "cradle" books? They were large, thick, awkward folios and quartos, scorned by book lovers of the period, who rushed to have them rubricated and illuminated in the manner of the medieval manuscript.

Type Faces

Incunabula were printed from type faces designed and cut by the early printers. Type faces tended to be large, loose, black and bold. It was not until the 16th century that scholars, questioning or defending the tradition of the ages, awakened the people of Europe to the value of books as instruments of knowledge. With this renaissance came a demand not only for more books but for better printed books with type faces which were simple, clear, delicate and artistic. The 16th century has been rightly called the Golden Age of Typography. In succeeding centuries type designers, seeking to create new type faces with style and beauty, returned to this Golden Age for inspiration.

No attempt will be made in this brief review of incunabula to clarify such terms as matrices, fonts, punches, patrices or chases. The designing and cutting of type faces and the intricacy of the printing operations are a story in themselves.

The Title Page

        The first title page used in an incunabulum was a colo-
phon, placed not at the beginning but at the end of the book.
In addition to the title, author, publisher, and occasionally
the date, the finishing stroke of the colophon was usually the
printer's mark.

        The first separate title page did not appear until 1463.
Soon the printers began to decorate the title page with huge
initial letters, with profuse printer's flowers, with heavy
wood-cut borders and with descriptive titles containing as
many as 90 words.   Many years later, John Baskerville, an
English printer, designed the "perfect" title page.   In his
edition of Virgil, the title page was simple, unornamented,
and balanced in every detail of print and space--a model for
future title pages.

        The modern title page--the door to the book--tends to
strive for an artistic balance, with the weight of the type at
the top of the page, with no great diversity in type face and
with little crowding of material.   The verso (back) of the
title page carries information that the early printers would
not recognize--the copyright statement, details on the various
printings, Library of Congress classification numbers, even
cataloging information for libraries.

        A double-page spread is occasionally used for title
pages by book designers, but even with the use of color,
many of these pages have resulted in waste space, a maze
of vertical and horizontal lines and a tangle of type faces.

        In modern books the titles are suggestive rather than
descriptive, seeking to express the essence of the book and
to arouse the interest of the potential reader--for example:
Thomas Wolfe's poignant You Can't Go Home Again and the
dramatic story of the New York Times entitled The Power
and the Glory.

The Illustrations

        The incunabula were illustrated by wood cuts, engrav-
ings and printer's ornaments.

        It was not until 15 years after books were printed by
movable type that wood cuts were used as illustration, al-

though the art was well known long before. The first book
with wood cut illustration was printed by Albrecht Pfister.
The simple pictures were in outline, with the expectation that
the designs were to be hand-colored.

A master of the art of the wood cut was Albrecht
Dürer. He began his work the year Columbus sailed west
to discover the East. The magnificent intricacies of his illustrations are best exemplified in Apocalypse.

Perhaps the most popular book with woodcut illustrations was the huge Nuremberg Chronicle, printed in 1493.
Brief biographies of famous men were accompanied by portraits. That the same pictures were used for several different men appeared to trouble the printers not at all. In
short, three kings of three different countries looked exactly
alike!

Engravings on copper plates, usually done by the gold-
smiths, were found to be quite impossible to reproduce in
the printing process. For a time the art was abandoned;
then it was discovered that the engraving could be done on a
separate sheet which could be tipped into its proper place in
the book. An early engraved illustration pictured Caxton,
the printer, kneeling to present his first book to Margaret,
Duchess of Burgundy as she stood in her chamber surrounded
by her ladies.

Book ornamentation in the incunabula was achieved
largely by the use of color laid on by hand and by printer's
flowers, simple designs repeated to form blocks of decoration often extending to heavy borders.

An incunabulum may indeed be a far cry from a modern book, printed on glossy paper and illustrated with full
page photographs in color. But the comparison in no way
dims the importance of incunabula in the story of the printed
book. Scholars study them and collectors bid fabulous sums
to own one. Closely guarded in the British Museum and
Pierpont Morgan Library are collections of many hundreds
of incunabula--legacies of the past and legacies to the future.

PRINTING SPREADS ACROSS EUROPE

As the art of printing by movable type spread from

Germany across the Alps to Italy, back to Germany, to
France, to the Low Countries and to England, it is scarcely
possible in a brief summary to pay tribute to the hundreds of
printers who helped to move Europe into the Renaissance.
Four printers are considered here in the light of their unusual contributions to the change and growth in the art of
printing by movable type.

John Fust and Peter Schoeffer of Mainz

An old legend claimed that John Fust was in league
with the Devil.   When Fust and his partner, Peter Schoeffer,
became book publishers and issued the first publisher's catalog of 21 titles, Fust decided to peddle his books to the citizens of Paris.   Printing by movable type was then unknown
in France.   Fust was called a magician and was cast into
prison.   He was even accused of using his own blood to paint
the red letters in the books.   To free himself from prison,
he was forced to disclose the "secret" of printing by movable
type.

Such a tale does not dim the significance of their
printing art.   The wondrous Mainz Psalter, the first dated
book printed by movable type, was done in the printing plant
of Fust and Schoeffer.   A colophon at the end of the book
gave the date, 1457, and the name of the printer.   Beneath
the colophon appeared the first printer's mark, a device used
by a printer to identify his work and to publicize his titles,
much as "Put a tiger in your tank" was used by Exxon.

The customs of using printer's marks in books is
still common.   Books published by Knopf have the "mark" of
the Borzoi hound; a shield bearing an ancient press and the
initials G. P. P. S. identify G. P. Putnam Sons.

The Fust and Schoeffer printer's mark consisted of
two black shields hanging from a tree branch.   Strange white
markings which may have been printer's tools were inter-
posed on the shields.   There was no motto.   An appropriate
one might have been the 42-line Bible on one shield and the
Mainz Psalter on the other shield.

Aldus Manutius of Venice, Italy

Three years after Columbus discovered America, Aldus

went to Venice to learn the printing trade.   He had been a
tutor of Latin and Greek in a Royal House.

Aldus, the master in his printing house, made an unusual black ink, bought the finest papers and proofread for
errors.   He strove for perfection in his printed books through
a faultless combination of paper, text, type and illustration.
His most famous book, Hypnerotomachia Poliphili (A Dream
of Love), is considered by some authorities to be the most
perfect book ever printed.

Books in the days of early printing were large, heavy
and awkward to carry.   In fact, in the universities the wealthy
students hired pages to lug their books.   Aldus printed a
series of small books to fit in one's pocket--many, many
years before our paperbacks.

Aldus also designed two most interesting fonts of type,
one of the Greek alphabet for the printing of his famous
Greek classics, and another of thin, crowded, slanted letters
known as italic.   Italic letters are often used within the text
of modern day books to emphasize a phrase or a book title.

Aldus had financial problems.   He was arrested once
as a spy and saw his printing plant burned to the ground.
His printer's mark, a ship's anchor with a dolphin entwined,
was most appropriate; its motto, "Make haste slowly," epito-
mized Aldus' printing career.

The House of Aldus stood for 100 years.   Aldus' body
lies in a church near his printing plant.

William Caxton of Westminster, England

Born in England, Caxton became a cloth merchant in
London.   Sent to the Low Countries to trade, he soon was
made "Governor" of the Merchant Adventurers in Bruges,
Belgium.   Later, he entered the service of the Duke and
Duchess of Burgundy.   The Duchess, who greatly prized her
collection of illuminated manuscripts, became interested in
this new art of printing.   At her request, Caxton learned
the craft and presented to the Duchess his first printed
book--The Recuyell of the Histories of Troye.

Caxton, in time, returned to England and opened a
printing shop "at the sign of the red pale," near Westminster

Abbey. Unfortunately, Caxton was not a good printer. His
books were ugly, with poor paper, almost unreadable, high-
pointed types, ragged lines, uneven margins, no capital letters, no punctuation, no title page. If there wasn't room at
the end of a line to complete a word, Caxton broke off the
word, as wo for woman.

        But forgotten is the poor printing. Caxton will be re-
membered as the first printer to print, not in Latin but in
the vernacular (English), and to issue English classics for
English people to read and enjoy, among them Chaucer's
Canterbury Tales and Malory's Morte d'Arthur. In 1911
Pierpont Morgan paid $42,000 for a copy of Morte d'Arthur
printed by Caxton. Today it is priceless.

        The printer's mark used by Caxton bore no motto.
Rather it consisted of a large WC (William Caxton), with SC
in smaller letters probably standing for "sancta Cologne"
where he learned the printing trade. The finishing stroke
is 74, very likely for the year 1474 in which he began to
print.

Christopher Plantin, Antwerp, Belgium

        Plantin was not his real name. Fearing that the dis-
tinguished name of his adopted parents would be soiled by a
connection with a questionable career in printing, Christopher
assumed the name Plantin after the weed, plantain.

        Plantin, however, needed no apology for his career.
He was a scholar who spoke, read and wrote French, Spanish, German, Flemish, English, Latin and Italian. As printer to the King and to the University of Leyden, Plantin's
printing house was extensive, with 22 presses, 150 workmen
and 73 fonts of type.

        Lost at sea in a great storm was Plantin's most
famous printed book, The Polyglot Bible. Printed on vellum
in eight volumes and in four different languages (the word
polyglot means many languages), the Bible was commissioned
by King Philip II of Spain who agreed to pay Plantin the
equivalent of $34,000 for it. Early printing was a precari-
ous business.

        The artist Rubens, who was befriended by Plantin, de-
signed the printer's mark--a hand coming out of a cloud, hold-

ing a golden compass.   An intertwined ribbon bore the motto,
"Labor with Constancy. "

Plantin had seven daughters and no sons.   After his
death and burial in Antwerp Cathedral, his son-in-law continued the work of the printing house.

Visitors to Antwerp may now see, recreated in the
Plantin Museum, an ancient and authentic printing house with
beautiful furniture, tapestries, original canvases by Rubens
and all the early printing equipment.

A camel caravan loaded with silks, spices and playing
cards printed by xylography--a rude image print of St. Christopher carrying the Christ Child across a river--a glorious
42-line Bible--an ugly printing of the tales of King Arthur
and his knights--an exquisite Aldine and a "pocket book":
this listing may be considered a thumbnail sketch of printing
in Europe.   Standing in the shadows were the printers who,
with inventive genius, with tenacity and with scholarly intent,
made books available as Europe emerged from the medieval
age.   The printed page was the gift Europe gave to America.

PRINTING IN THE WESTERN WORLD

In America the printing press crossed the jungles of
Mexico to Christianize the natives.   It passed through storms
at sea to follow the Pilgrims into their new world.   It moved
with the flat boats down the Ohio and Mississippi rivers; with
the axe and the plow into prairie country; with the covered
wagons westward across the mountain passes.   In Europe
printing was introduced to an awakening civilization.   In
America, printing was a pioneer adventure in the wilderness.

Printing in Mexico

Several European countries did not have a printing
press when Juan Kromberger, a leading Spanish printer, sent
a "printing expedition" to Mexico in the year 1539.   Juan
Pablos was the printer, his mission to print religious tracts
for the Christianization of the natives.   He was required by
Cromberger to cross the ocean under sail with a printing
press; to assemble it; to set up shop with all necessary materials (type, paper and ink); to print 3000 sheets daily; to

accept no salary, and to print for ten years under Cromberger's name.

Pablos printed only eight titles. This first printing
on the continent of America was poorly done--uneven type
faces smudged with ink blots, and deep, dirty borders of
printer's flowers* on a page which also bore a Cardinal's
hat as a printer's mark.

Pablos' first book, Breve y mas compendiosa doctrina
christiana, printed in 1539, might well be called an American
incunabulum. Either the natives read the tracts "to pieces"
or they found other uses for the paper; at any rate, very few
books from the press in Mexico City are in existence today.

In Colonial America

One hundred years after Pablos printed in Mexico, a
printing press came to the Massachusetts Bay Colony. Josiah
Glover, an early settler, was determined to establish a college for the training of ministers in the New World. He
sailed back to England, collected a small sum of money, and
bought a press, paper and ink. With Stephen Day and his
two sons, who were apprenticed printers, Glover and his
family began the journey back to the Colony. But Glover
died of smallpox during the voyage.

The first printing press in Colonial America was owned
and managed by Glover's widow. Later, Ann Franklin and
Dinah Nuthead also ran print shops--a distinct departure from
the European tradition of male printers.

The Cambridge Press. The first titles printed by the
Cambridge Press (so named by Mrs. Glover) were The Free-
man's Oath, An Almanac for 1639, and the Whole Booke of
Psalmes.

If, one day, a half sheet of paper, headed The Freeman's Oath, slides out of an old book in the family attic,
cherish it. As of now, no copies of the original printing of
The Freeman's Oath are in existence.

---

*Printer's flowers are small designs repeated many times
to form a pattern for a border or to balance a page of
type.

An almanac and a Bible were the books most commonly found in the homes of the early settlers.   The almanac
was usually attached by a string to the kitchen door.   By
the decrees of the almanac, crops were planted and journeys
made.   No copies of the Almanac printed by the Cambridge
Press are extant, as they were literally "used up."

The Whole Booke of Psalmes faithfully Translated into
English Metre ... Imprinted 1640 is commonly called the Bay
Psalm Book.   This first book of Scriptures to be printed in
what is now the United States was comprised of 147 crudely
printed leaves with a title page crammed with a 90-word
résumé of the book and decorated with printer's flowers.

Only ten copies of the Bay Psalm Book are in existence today.   Four copies are in perfect condition and are
worth a king's ransom.

John Eliot.   The next important book to be printed in
Colonial America was John Eliot's Indian Bible.   Eliot had
worked as a missionary among the Indians and had translated the Bible into the Indian language in an effort to bring
the Christian faith to the Indians.   Eliot sought a printer
capable of cutting a font of Indian characters.   Marmaduke
Johnson was sent from England to solve the many problems
connected with the printing of the Indian Bible.   In 1663 the
first copy appeared titled as:

UP-BIBLUM GOD
NANEESWE
NUKKONE TESTAMENT
KAH WONK
WUSKU TESTAMENT

A copy of this Bible was purchased by Isaiah Thomas,
a colonial printer, for $7--a fabulous sum in those days.
Thomas's copy is preserved in the library of the American
Antiquarian Society at Worcester, Massachusetts.

Early Newspapers.   As the wilderness was slowly
conquered, printing in Colonial America remained at a low
ebb, narrow in content and poor in execution.   However, a
trend in printing, peculiar to the New World, was emerging,
namely the newspaper.

The first newspapers to be printed were the Boston
Gazette (1719) and the New England Courant (1921).   The

Gazette was issued only when there was a "glut of news."
The British colonial rulers were quick to fine or imprison a
printer if he dared to print a disloyal statement. Hence,
newspapers contained little local news, being content to print,
in a dull fashion, the local laws and warmed-over news from
the mother country. Not until the seeds of the Revolution
were sown did newspapers begin to play a significant role.
One such was the Massachusetts Spy, printed by Isaiah Thomas.

     The editor and printer of the New England Courant,
issued in 1721, was James Franklin, an anti-Royalist and a
man of fickle temper. To his shop came a nine-year-old
apprentice--his brother Benjamin.

     Benjamin Franklin. Apprenticed for nine years, Ben-
jamin received no money, but was clothed and fed by his
cruel master, who often beat him and forced him to stand
for long hours setting type by hand. Benjamin persevered.
He borrowed books and often slipped under his brother's door
clever notes and comments which James printed as his own.

     James, after repeated warnings from the Royal Gov-
ernor, continued to print in his newspaper scornful statements about the British rule in the colonies. He was jailed.
For a time his wife, Ann, and young Benjamin continued to
print the newspaper. But Benjamin grew more and more unhappy and one day ran away to seek employment with William
Bradford, a printer in Philadelphia.

     An amusing and often-told tale concerns Franklin's
arrival in Philadelphia. Hungry after his journey, he bought
three rolls of bread. With a roll under each arm and eating
the third, he walked down the street, the pockets of his great
coat bulging with his personal belongings. A young woman
laughed long at this strange spectacle. Benjamin Franklin
later married her.

     Industrious and friendly, Franklin soon won recogni-
tion from the Royal Governor, who asked Franklin for advice concerning the shabby printing being done in Philadelphia.
Knowing there was much to be learned from the English printers, Franklin went to London. For three years he worked
as an apprentice in an English printing house. Upon his return to Philadelphia, he established his own press.

     The Pennsylvania Gazette and Poor Richard's Almanac

were Franklin's most famous imprints. Delighted readers of
the Pennsylvania Gazette were made aware of the fact that a
newspaper could be a source of entertainment. With the publication of the Almanac, wit for the first time colored the
contents of books printed in colonial days. The Almanac became a "best seller." Ten thousand copies were sold yearly
and each new issue was eagerly awaited. Many of Franklin's
wise sayings which first appeared in the Almanac are quoted
today.

Franklin's last will and testament began, "I, Benjamin Franklin, printer." He might well have begun it with
the words, "I, Benjamin Franklin, diplomat, scientist, inventor, statesman." But he evidently considered printing
his greatest achievement in life.

Isaiah Thomas. A newspaper, The Massachusetts Spy,
was printed by Isaiah Thomas, a staunch patriot. His deter-
mination to free the colonists from English rule was so vehe-
mently expressed that the Royal Governor ordered him to
leave Boston. In the dead of night, Thomas hurried his
presses to Worcester, Massachusetts and continued to cry
out for independence from English rule. The Spy played a
major role in bringing the Revolutionary War nearer.

Thomas also believed that the books printed at that
time for children were dismal. The stories threatened children, warning them that to die happily they must live pure
and somber lives. Realizing that children needed books for
this world, rather than the next, Thomas gave them The New
England Primer, The Blue Backed Speller and a series of
"tokens and garlands" not unlike the English Chapbooks.
Isaiah Thomas was a historian, a printer, a publisher and
a proprietor of book stores with branches as far west in the
wilderness as Albany, New York.

John Peter Zenger. Of the "four freedoms" cherished
today, freedom of the press is perhaps the most abused and
the most controversial. However, colonial printers had no
such freedom, being liable to a prison sentence if what they
printed was contrary to the decree of a Royal Governor. In
modern parlance, the colonial press was shackled and arbi-
trarily censored.

This aspect of the struggle for freedom culminated
in the arrest and imprisonment of John Peter Zenger. He
and his partner, William Bradford, had published in the New

York Weekly Journal articles attacking the Royal Governor of New York. The Governor demanded that Zenger be tried for libel. Zenger was defended so eloquently by the distinguished lawyer, Alexander Hamilton, that he was acquitted. No longer could the news be censored and the newspaper proceeded to fire many a volley in the war for independence.

After the Revolution, as State after State was carved out of the wilderness, the first printing in each State was usually a newspaper. Wherever the settlers went, the press followed. Printers lived a rugged pioneer existence, their printing shop sometimes a tent pitched at a dusty crossroad.

The newspaper played a most significant role in the development of a new nation "conceived in liberty." It is, indeed, a long, long road from a flimsy sheet of "news" struck off on a hand press to the modern printing plant of a newspaper, the presses driven by computers and the news from around the world flashed by satellite.

Did these pioneering printers dream as they pulled down the handle of a printing press that 500 years later the largest and best equipped printing plant in the world--the Government Printing Office, of the United States--would in one year issue 650,000,000 copies of its publications?

STOP AND THINK

As you have read this chapter you have been involved in the miracle of print. The next time you buy a paperback, indulge in a flashback, as in the movies, and in your mind's eye see:

A wood carver in China laboring to cut a Chinese character.

The magnificent Diamond Sutra, the masterpiece of xylography (printing by means of wood blocks).

A caravan crossing to Europe carrying playing cards printed by xylography.

A curious European scholar carefully examining this new process, and adapting it for the making of image prints and block books.

Johann Gutenberg as he worked for many years in sec-
recy to perfect printing by movable type, only to have
his ultimate triumph, the beautiful 42-line Bible,
snatched from him and printed by John Fust and Peter
Schoeffer.

The activity in the great printing houses of Aldus Manutius, Christopher Plantin and William Caxton, who
pioneered in the awakening of Europe.

The early printed books (1450-1501 A.D.) known as in-
cunubula, in which the printers gave the book the shape
and form it still has today.

Juan Pablos, who set up a printing press in Mexico City
and printed the first book on the continent of America,
his purpose to Christianize the natives.

An early Colonial American newspaper in which were
sown the seeds of the Revolution and which later helped
to spread printing to the new West.   Benjamin Franklin
as he fashioned a homely Almanac, and Peter Zenger
who championed freedom of the press in a new world.

Look again at that paperback you just bought.   Between its covers it may hold hours of fascinating reading.
But also between its covers it holds all the magic of the inventive minds which labored to give the world the gift of the
printed word.

SUGGESTED ACTIVITIES

Field Trips

Words and pictures may faithfully describe a printing
press, but to see the entire process of gathering, writing
and printing the news will really bring to life what you have
read in this chapter.

Ask your librarian to arrange a field trip for you and
your classmates to a newspaper or book publishing plant.

Then, why not write under your own byline an article
about your trip for the school newspaper?

Research Papers

Some suggestions for special credit research papers:

The beginnings of printing in China and its spread to Europe.   (Be sure to include the history of playing cards.)

Great books printed by the houses of Aldus, Caxton and Plantin.

The most popular book in Colonial America--an Almanac. (Make use of your local museum and include the Farmer's Almanac.)

Displays and Exhibits

The story of printing lends itself to displays and exhibits.   Possible sources of materials are: 1) Commercial exhibits--use the indexes for free and inexpensive materials; 2) Transparencies--make your own; the book by Laurence Wroth listed in the supplementary readings will be of help to you: 3) Clippings and pictures--the library files will yield illustrative materials on the subject; 4) Field trip materials --newspaper and book publishing plants are usually generous with materials if they are assured of your interest; 5) Community resources files--consult these files for business concerns, museums and book collectors who might loan materials.

FURTHER READING

Carter, Thomas F.   The Invention of Printing in China and Its Spread Westward.   2nd ed.   New York: Ronald, 1955.
        Exactly what the title says.   Chapter 1 is most important.   You may find the subject of playing cards and paper money, first printed in China, worth pursuing on your own.

McMurtrie, Douglas C.   Wings For Words.   Chicago: Rand McNally, 1940.
        The life of Johann Gutenberg written for young people, by an author who knows printing from A to Z.   Note in Chapter 3 under Further Readings that The Book by McMurtrie

is listed.   It is valuable reading for this chapter too.   High-
lighted are unusual aspects of the printed book--incunabula,
block books, title pages, printers' marks and printing in
early America.   Illustrated.

Winship, George Parker.   Gutenberg to Plantin.   Cambridge:
    Harvard University Press, 1930.
        If the great tasks which had to be accomplished by
the early printers intrigue you, then here is a brief and
simple account of their victories and defeats.

Wroth, Lawrence C.   A History of the Printed Book, being
    the third number of The Dolphin.   New York: Limited
    Editions Club, 1938.
        A very large book, crammed with pictures that help
you to explore the history of printing.   The author was a
distinguished collector of Americana for the John Carter
Brown Library at Brown University.

Chapter 8

JOURNEYS TO GREAT BOOK SHRINES
OF THE WORLD

"Is there anybody there?" said
the Traveller,
Knocking on the moonlit door. "
--Walter de la Mare

The snows of Kilimanjaro. The coral reefs of Tahiti.
The Land of the Midnight Sun. The South Pole. Enticing
lands within reach, insists the travel agent. He will also
plan an itinerary that takes you to the Pierpont Morgan Library, the Folger Shakespeare Library, the British Museum
and the Vatican Library.

PREPARATION FOR A JOURNEY

Prepare for this bibliographical tour. See that you
have proper introductions to the Keeper of the Books, librarians, book dealers, even an Embassy or two. Remind
yourself that no pen, no umbrella, no brief case should be
taken into these magnificent collections. But do take information gleaned from reading prior to your visit, for the
"eye sees only what it knows. "

Be assured that your welcome will be a cold one if
you visit a certain part of the Vatican Library and stupidly
ask, "Where are the books?"; if you should inquire as to the
value of an urn on a mantelpiece in the Folger Shakespeare
Library; if you are told that an author, seated day after day
at the same desk in the British Museum, is writing a classic
novel and you reply, "How odd"; or if you remark, "Oh, pretty" when you are shown the Della Robbia relief over a door-

way in the Pierpont Morgan Library. So don't start off gaily
some morning to conquer the world of museums and libraries
without careful preparation.

After your return from a first journey, plan other
journeys to include the libraries of Harvard University, the
New York Public Library, the Library of Congress, the Bodleian, the Bibliothèque Nationale and, for contrast, a little
Carnegie Library tucked away in the hills of Pennsylvania.

THE BRITISH MUSEUM
LONDON, ENGLAND

Museums had their beginning in the shrines built a-
bout 500 B.C. in honor of the mythological nine Muses. The
shrines became repositories of gifts, temples of art or collections of objects testifying to man's desire to please or
appease the gods.

In the Christian era, the churches housed religious
relics--a finger of a Saint or the robe of a Prophet. With
these relics might also be displayed ostrich eggs, the skin
of a gorilla or other memorabilia from faraway lands--a miniature museum. Later, a gentleman's house contained his
cabinet, a small room in which were gathered curiosities.
Galleries, imitating the Grand Gallery of the Louvre, Paris,
were devoted to a collection of books, paintings and sculpture.
The cabinet and the gallery gradually merged to form the
museum.

Early museums were often assembled by kings and
emperors. The Escorial in Spain under Philip II was a library, a museum, a monastery, a palace, a hospital and a
university. With the recognition that the museum might aid
in the dissemination of new knowledge in the arts and sciences, they were made public in the 18th and 19th centuries.
The Ashmolean Museum at Oxford, England is considered to
be the first of the historic museums.

An early museum was likely to be scornfully dubbed
"An Ark of Novelties," crowded with "believe it or not"
items and littered with dust-laden jars containing insects and
human organs. The modern museum beggars this description. For example, the Museum of Natural History in New
York City, visited each year of thousands of people, is an

institution of learning with intelligently arranged displays,
dioramas of animals in their native habitats, dinosaur skele-
tons, exquisite jewels and the eternal calendar of planets
moving about the sun.

The Founding of "The Greatest Library in the World"

The story of the British Museum begins with its
"ghosts": John Keats viewing with great sadness the Elgin
Marbles; Karl Marx reading in the Round Room; the historian
Macaulay writing hour after hour at his table in the King's
Library; Colin Wilson spreading out his sleeping bag; Baron
Corvo taking baths in the cloak room; and over and among
them all, striding the tyrant Panizzi, Keeper of Books.

In 1753, the British Museum was made public and
national. Standing in the shadows were its true founders;
Sir Robert Cotton, Robert Harley, Earl of Oxford, and Sir
Hans Sloane.

The Cottonian Collection. Of the three collections
that of Sir Robert Cotton was considered the most priceless.
Among the rarities were The Lindisfarne Gospels, the Anglo-
Saxon Chronicle, and the Magna Charta. But the British
government was extremely lax in the care of the collection
and allowed it to gather dust on crowded shelves. Finally,
the collection was moved to Ashburnham House where a dis-
astrous fire occurred. Only a few scraps remain of one of
the rarest of the manuscripts--the Cottonian Genesis.

The Harleian Collection. Robert Harley, the Earl of
Oxford, collected in the "grand manner," with emphasis on
fine bindings. His son added to the collection, which eventually included 8,000 volumes of manuscripts, 50,000 printed
books, 400,000 pamphlets, 40,000 prints, coins and medals.
Purchased by the British government, neither the Harleian
nor the Cottonian collection was adequately housed.

Sloaniana. A physician, a natural scientist, a traveler, Sir Hans Sloane collected plants, fruits, corals, min-
erals, stones, earth, shells, animals and insects. To this
collection, housed in Great Russell Street, Sloane added coins,
medals, drawings, paintings, books and manuscripts. Visitors came from all over the world, among them Benjamin
Franklin and Frederick Handel. Handel angered Sir Hans by
placing his buttered muffin on one of the rare volumes.

Montague House. These three imposing collections
were the foundation stones of the British Museum. With an
Act of Parliament on June 7, 1853, The British Museum
came into existence.

Montague House was chosen as a repository for the
scattered collections. The paneled entrance hall, lined with
glass cabinets, and the Grand Staircase, complete with three
stuffed giraffes tipping their heads on the ceiling above a
landing, were reminiscent of a French palace. Galleries
were added, straggling off the main house, and after four
years of planning the Museum was opened to visitors.

Admission to Montague House was a complicated procedure. The visitor had first to present himself at the
porter's lodge, fill in forms, be scrutinized by the Librarian
and then wait for days for tickets. Children were not ad-
mitted. For fifty years these rules were unchanged.

Growth and Change

Due to a flood of acquisitions by gift and by purchase,
the Museum grew. The Thomason tracts were added. Every
small book, pamphlet and newspaper published in London, in
the provinces or abroad, if in English, was collected and
preserved by the bookseller, George Thomason, in a time of
national strife and crisis. Many of the 22,255 pieces were
hidden by Thomason in false table tops to avoid seizure and
Thomason himself played the role of a modern 007 double
agent.

Antiquities of inestimable value--the Rosetta Stone, a
key to Egyptian culture, and the Elgin Marbles, the glory of
Greek sculpture--became a part of the collection.

Montague House was now entirely inadequate, and
after 50 years of planning and construction a new British
Museum, a "Temple of Art," rose on the present site near
St. Paul's Cathedral in London. The building, from the
Ionic columns to the decorative iron railings, was an articu-
late lecture on architectural design.

Sir Anthony Panizzi

It was the appointment of Sir Anthony Panizzi as

Principal Librarian that changed the Museum into a library.
Considered a tyrant by some, he resolved to make the library
the finest in the world and to remove from the Museum the
clutter of the natural science specimens.   Macaulay wrote
that Panizzi would at any time give mammoths for an Aldine
(a book from the presses of Aldus Manutius, Venetian printer
and publisher).

Panizzi's grand plan called for more government funds
to buy foreign books; a copyright law that would force publishers to deliver directly to the door of the British Museum
copies of all British books; and an augmented staff to provide
better service to readers.   During the next 30 years, as a
result of Panizzi's vision and direction, the number of printed
books rose to 1,500,000, and 180,000 readers had used the
library.

But Panizzi was greatly distressed at the overcrowd-
ing of the book collection, much of which was stacked on the
floor or jammed three deep on the library shelves.   As plans
for the expansion of the library were considered, the idea of
a Round Reading Room became a reality and in 1857 the
great copper-covered done, rising over the Reading Room,
became one of the sights of London.   The dome, carried on
cast iron ribs, provided 1-1/4 million cubic feet of space
and 25 miles of shelving.   Like the spokes of a great wheel,
the handsome desks and well-designed, mahogany chairs
stretched out from a central service desk.

This arrangement has been widely copied.   Perhaps
you have seen the great circular Reading Room in the Library
of Congress, Washington, D. C.

A National Library

Since the beginning of the 1920s the Museum has found
itself in one crisis after another, due to fund shortages and
inadequate housing.   Great stores of archeological "finds"
were still packed in boxes in warehouses.   Hitler's bombs
did much damage to the Museum although the Elgin Marbles
and other rarities were hidden in a stone quarry in the countryside or sandbagged in tunnels beneath London.   In the en-
suing years scholars feared that the Museum would never be
restored to its former glory.

But plans were submitted to the government for a new

building in a more favorable location, for the complete separa-
tion of the Museum and the Library, and for a change of
name.   In 1970 Parliament agreed to spend 36 million pounds
on a possible relocation, and the rebuilding of what is to be
known as the National Library.

Among the Treasures

So great in numbers and so priceless are the treasures
of the British Museum that it is difficult to select a few of
them for special mention.   But to know that these treasures
are there in safekeeping, to be allowed to see a few on a
guided tour or on exhibition, strengthens a belief in the stead-
fastness of man's devotion to the arts.   Among the treasures
are:

The Cottonian Genesis--a few charred fragments of a
Bible in Greek.

The Rosetta Stone--the key to Egyptian hieroglyphic
writing.

Papyrus rolls--excavations from the buried city of Herculaneum.   A gift from Queen Victoria to the Museum.

The Magna Charta--England's Declaration of Independence.

The Diamond Sutra--first dated book printed in China
on wood blocks.

The Lindisfarne Gospels--early illuminated manuscript,
rivaling the Book of Kells.

The Chronicles of Geoffrey of Monmouth--a record of
everyday life in early England.   The first English "newspaper."

Beowulf--a copy of the English epic, dated 1000 A.D.

The Codex Sinaiticus--an early Bible in Greek (a Septuagint) bound by Douglas Cockerell.

Magnificent illuminated manuscripts: Queen Mary's
Psalter, the Bedford Book of Hours, the Sforza Book
of Hours.

Ars Moriendi (The Art of Dying)--a block book.

Christmas Carols--from the Burney music collection.

Americana--issues of the New England Courant published by a very young Benjamin Franklin.

Add or subtract, multiply or divide, the glory of the British Museum is unchallenged.

THE FOLGER SHAKESPEARE LIBRARY
WASHINGTON, D. C.

When he was a young man, Henry Clay Folger purchased, for one dollar and twenty-five cents, a facsimile of a First Folio of Shakespeare. This Folio became the corner stone of a life passion.

The Building

The Folger Shakespeare Library was built "not to sit in grandeur but to be used." Mr. Folger's ambition was to construct a library reminiscent of Shakespeare's time. But such a structure could hardly be placed next to the Library of Congress and the cold majesty of the Supreme Court building.

A white Georgian marble building rose on the site, its facade centered in nine panel sculptures depicting scenes from Shakespeare's plays. High on the facade were carved Mr. Folger's favorite quotations from Shakespeare. A terrace set with massive marble benches led to the main entrance of the Library. On the west front was the delightful garden fountain with the figure of Puck, sculptured by Brenda Putnam. The pedestal bears the words, "Lord, what fooles these mortals be."

Within the building, England of the 16th and 17th centuries comes alive, and the Shakespearean scholar finds himself in most congenial surroundings. The great Exhibition Room has oak-paneled walls, a high ceiling decorated with strap work, a floor with designs appropriate to the theme of the building, heavy floor candelabra, glass display cases, paintings and statuary. Over the doors are the coats of arms of the United States and of Queen Elizabeth I.   The heraldic arms of Shakespeare decorate an exterior balcony.

The Theatre is in the traditional manner of those in which Shakespeare's comedies and tragedies were played. An inner, outer and upper stage, a side gallery, the walls of stone and rough plaster and a flagstone floor contribute to the 16th century atmosphere.   There is no pit.

At one end of the Reading Room is a stained glass window which depicts the Seven Ages of Man from As You Like It.   A huge marble fireplace dominates the room.   Two tiers of wall shelving, the upper level reached by a balcony and stairs, extend to a high beamed ceiling.   The room has the quiet dignity of a private library.

The building stands as a shrine not only to Shakespeare but to the Elizabethan Age.

The Donor

The life of a dedicated scholar began for Henry Clay Folger (1857-1930) when he discovered as a student at Amherst College that his greatest interest was in English literature.   Inspired by Ralph Waldo Emerson, young Folger came to believe that Shakespeare was the world's outstanding genius and to that belief he dedicated his life and his fortune.

After graduating from Amherst College Mr. Folger entered the Law School at Columbia College, receiving his law degree cum laude.   But instead of a career in law he turned his full attention to business.   In a few years he became president of the Standard Oil Company of New York and later the Chairman of the Board.   Upon retirement and until his death in 1930 (two weeks after the corner stone of the Library was laid), he devoted himself to the collection of Shakespeareana.

Mrs. Folger shared his enjoyment of Shakespeare and his interest in book collecting, and it is fitting that the portraits of both Folgers hang side by side on a memorial screen in the Reading Room.

In Mr. Folger's will, the Trustees of Amherst College were given "ownership in trust" of the building and the collection, their task being to perpetuate the founder's intent that

this historical collection, devoted to the civilization of the
16th-17th centuries with a focus on Shakespeare, be open to
all scholars.

Mr. Folger was a quiet man, bent on a great adventure. The reward, while in a measure his, was in truth
bestowed upon the Shakespearean scholar.

The Collection

Among the dramatic items in the collection are:
Shakespearean play bills numbering two hundred and fifty
thousand; Hamlet in eight hundred different editions; Shakespeare's signature to legal documents; and personal relics--
a piece of wood from Shakespeare's birth room and furniture
from Ann Hathaway's cottage. But the collection is not concerned with "curiosities." Such an emphasis would be un-
worthy of the depth, breadth and variety of the collection
which to this day continues to a "full perfection. "

Based on the belief that Shakespeare could not be
studied in a vacuum, the collection re-creates a social history of England from 1450 to 1700. Scholars come not only
to write, study and research minute facets of Shakespeare's
plays, poetry and sonnets, but to understand the times in
which he lived.

Mindful that an inexpensive facsimile of the First
Folio* of Shakespeare was the incentive for his collecting,
Mr. Folger gathered 79 First Folios out of the 200 copies
extant.   Of the Second, Third and Fourth Folios many are
association copies which belonged to royalty, to actors and
to distinguished men of letters.   Other rarities are a first
edition of Shakespeare's earliest published play and a 1604
edition of Hamlet.

Equally notable are books which Shakespeare used for
reference in the writing of his plays; books in which Shakespeare's plays are mentioned or analyzed; books on music
in his plays; books bearing on Shakespeare's influence on
other writers; and modern editions of Shakespeare translated in many languages.

---

*A folio is a book of large size whose pages are formed by
folding the printed sheet once only.

Most fascinating are books and memorabilia concerning the Shakespeare theatre; prompt books; play bills; actor's costumes; pictures of actors who appeared in the plays; stage properties; modern Shakespeare festivals and productions at home and abroad.

Hundreds of association copies of Shakespeare's plays are treasured because many famous men and women wrote comments in the margins and underlined favorite passages. Of special interest are association copies which belonged to George Bernard Shaw, Queen Victoria and Abraham Lincoln.

In the vocabulary of the book collector, desired attributes of rare books and manuscripts include: uncut, original binding, mint condition, only copy known, first edition. Judged by these standards the Folger Library stands supreme.

Scholars agree with Dr. Rosenbach, a distinguished modern book collector, that the collection of Shakespeareana in the Folger Library is the finest that the world has known.

BIBLIOTHECA VATICANUS
VATICAN CITY, ITALY

Lying within the city of Rome is a miniature state of 106 acres, known as Vatican City. Here, in an apartment of the papal palace, lives the Pope, who governs the vast Holy Roman Catholic Church. Here also stands the largest and most imposing church in the world--St. Peter's. Founded on the "rock" of Christ's apostle, Peter, the church stands as a monument to the faith of the Catholic world.

A few thousand citizens live within Vatican City, where there is no business except for a tourist shop, no crime, no taxes. The private secretary to the Pope or an artisan who mends the damaged leaves of manuscripts are typical of those who serve with quiet dedication.

A Mecca and a Shrine

Pilgrims and tourists walk across St. Peter's Square in small groups or, in triumphant masses, pack every inch of St. Peter's Square on Holy Days at the expected appearance of the Pope at the window of his apartment, or in magnificent procession.

The great Bernini columns reach out like embracing arms. Above, the many domes and the immense statues of Christ and his disciples add grandeur to the building.

As pilgrims enter the Church they see sunlight touching the High Altar under which are entombed the bones of St. Peter; the magnificent bronze doors guarded by the brilliantly clad Swiss in uniforms of red, yellow and blue; the Pieta, a Mother mourning her dead Son; a statue of St. Peter, his foot worn smooth by the kisses of the devout; three priceless paintings by Raphael; and a final touch of glory in the Sistine Chapel, with frescoes of the Creation and Last Judgment painted by Michelangelo and "aching with color." The Church itself is a benediction.

The scholar, however, seeking to verify an obscure fact, turns upon entering Vatican City, in a north-easterly direction from the Church, to the two buildings which house the Vatican Library.

In the antiquity and wealth of its manuscripts and books, this library ranks first among European libraries.

The Story of the Bibliotheca Vaticanus

Ancient manuscripts collected by early Popes when the papal seat was at Avignon and while wars raged over Europe mark the beginning of the Bibliotheca Vaticanus. The most famous of these early manuscripts, the Codex Amiatinus of the 4th century, "wandered" from the papal collection and later appeared in the library of Lorenzo de Medici--a sacrifice to greed and laxity.

Pope Nicholas V (1447-1455) was the creator of the Vatican Library. He spent many hours studying manuscripts which in the papal tradition had been kept partially intact as one Pope succeeded another. But Pope Nicholas V was not content with the collection. He sent copyists to monastic, cathedral and university libraries to reproduce important manuscripts, insisting that the copying be perfect, that only the finest of parchment be used, and that the bindings be of crimson velvet with silver clasps. At his death, the library had become a reality, although no suitable place had yet been found to house the manuscripts.

Pope Sixtus IV installed the collections in four beauti-

fully decorated rooms in the Vatican Palace. The manuscripts were chained to reading tables and a borrower was
denied their use or forced to vouch for their return by leaving a sum of money. However, the collection grew amazingly due to the efforts of two distinguished librarians, Bussi
and Platina.

Pope Leo X, the son of Lorenzo de Medici, held the
famous collection of his father in one hand and the manuscripts
of the Vatican in the other. Wisely he kept them apart.
While adding to the magnificent Medician library, he sent
scholars all over the world to copy and buy manuscripts for
the Vatican. The collection was increased by approximately
4,000 rare books and manuscripts.

A century later Pope Sixtus V realized that the library rooms were entirely too small. Fontana, the Pope's
architect, designed a new building. Within it was the Sixtine
Library, a beautiful room, elaborately decorated with frescoes, depicting the glory of books and the triumph of scholarship. Fifty years later the chains were removed from the
manuscripts and they were placed in painted wooden presses
within the great square columns which supported the room.
To many visitors this room is the Vatican Library.

The Bibliotheca Vaticanus grew as collections were
purchased in their entirety or given as gifts to the Holy
Father.

From the monastery of Bobbio, Italy, established by
Celtic monks, came priceless ancient manuscripts. The
magnificent collection of the Duke of Urbino and the Library
of Queen Christina of Sweden, rich in manuscripts of French
literature, were added.

At the fall of Constantinople, Byzantine manuscripts
and exiled Byzantine scholars poured into the Vatican Library.
The Borghese collection of 300 manuscripts, once belonging
to the Vatican and "removed" by the Borghese family from
the papal library at Avignon, were re-purchased. The Borgio
library consisting of 500 incunabula and hundreds of Hebrew
and Oriental manuscripts enriched the Vatican collections.
The growth of the library was monumental.

One distressing incident ended happily. The victorious
French under Napoleon in 1798 selected 500 of the most precious Vatican manuscripts and carried them off as spoils of

war to the Bibliothèque Nationale in Paris. Seventeen years
later the manuscripts were mostly restored to the Vatican
library.

Platina, the Prefect

A brilliant organizer, well aware of the diverse meth-
ods of acquiring manuscripts, Bartolomeo Platina brought to
the Vatican Library energy and vision comparable to that,
much later, of Panizzi of the British Museum. Exact directions were given for copying and illuminating. Strict rules for
borrowing were established. Platina lived in a room adjoin-
ing the library, and in addition to his scholarly responsibili-
ties he bought candles for lighting, wood for fires, brooms
for cleaning and fox tails for dusting. For his duties he received 112 silver ducats annually (ninety-two dollars) and the
title of Prefect.

The Modern Vatican Library

To attempt to number the collection in the Vatican
library would be folly. Up to 1930, the extent of the collection was unknown. Nor was the exact location of books and
manuscripts known. Scholars had to be content to wait nine
hours or nine days while a search was made for their re-
quested materials.

In 1930, due to the efforts of Father Erhle, the Prefect of the library, a complete reorganization and moderniza-
tion were planned. With financial help from the Carnegie En-
dowment for International Peace and with professional advice
of the staff of the Library of Congress at Washington, a new
library catalog was developed. Seven miles of steel shelving
were added and an old stable and mosaic factory, stripped
down to the original stone and marble foundation, were rebuilt to provide adequate quarters.

The Vatican library was no longer a "prison house of
books" but a vast storehouse of knowledge now accessible to
the world of scholarship.

The Treasures of the Bibliotheca Vaticanus

Among the rarest treasures of the Vatican library are

the Codex Vaticanus, a 4th century Old Testament; two manuscripts of Virgil, copied in the 4th and 5th centuries; the
largest book in the world, an Old Testament dated the 13th
century; the note books and scores of Palestrina, the greatest composer of church music; and a palimpsest of Cicero's
De Republica, an exciting discovery indeed.

The most precious possessions of the Vatican Library
may well be crucial documents under lock and key in the
Secret Archives--such as the application of England's King
Henry VIII for his divorce, and Codex 1181 which contains
the proceedings against Galileo, who was tried for heresy
because he dared to defend the theory that the sun, not the
earth, was the center of the universe.

When one considers the great libraries of the world,
one thinks first of the Vatican library. Its antiquities are
unrivaled.

THE PIERPONT MORGAN LIBRARY
NEW YORK CITY

In New York City, within the shadow of the Empire
State Building, stands a library and a museum. Built in
classic Greek style of fitted marble blocks is a building that
a Grand Duke or a Prince might envy. It is the Pierpont
Morgan Library. Mr. Morgan may have been dubbed a "robber baron," a miniature Lorenzo de Medici, a collector who
knew not what he was collecting, but the splendor of the
Pierpont Morgan Library refutes these clichés.

The Building and Its Collection

A visitor usually enters the library through the Exhibition Room rather than through the great bronze doors which
open into a rotunda separating the East Room from the West
Room. The Exhibition Room, the walls hung with magnificent
tapestries, the glass display cases filled with priceless literary treasures, is a gateway to a world of art and beauty.
Built in 1928, the Exhibition Room stands on the site of Mr.
Morgan's old home.

Reading like a book collector's fairy tale, the schedule
of exhibitions open to the public includes: rare illuminated

manuscripts, blazing with color, a collection surpassed only
by that of the British Museum; countless manuscripts of literary works autographed by the authors; early printed books
of great rarity, including the Hypnerotomachia Poliphili, an
exquisitely printed Aldine, and beautiful books illustrative of
the art of the masters of book binding.

The spacious East Room houses a "gentleman's library" on floor-to-ceiling shelves protected by heavy criss-
crossed bronze wires.   Majestic bronzes and art objects of
antiquity further enhance the beauty of the room.   A copy of
the Gutenberg Bible is usually on display.

Walls, once hung with red damask from the Chigi
Palace; rare paintings; a desk with gold fittings; cabinets of
decorated boxes; reliquaries; miniatures in jeweled frames;
bronzes; terra cotta and marble busts; priceless enamels;
glorious tapestries; a magnificent portable altar, dated 1150
A.D.; jeweled book covers; a marble mantle piece and a 16th
century carved ceiling lifted intact from an Italian palace make
Mr. Morgan's study, the West Room, an intimate reflection
of an "Age of Elegance." It was here that Mr. Morgan came
daily whenever he was in New York.   In this room gathered
the world's greatest financiers to break the panic of 1907.
It was here that his erudite librarian, Belle da Costa Green,
placed on his desk rare books which he must buy or lose to
other collectors.   Over the fireplace a portrait of Mr. Morgan still presides over the West Room.

Morgan, the Man, the Collector

The creator of this "jeweled casket" was as fascinating as his collection.   Pierpont Morgan came from five generations of wealthy Connecticut farmers.   Before his death
in 1931, he had been received by the German Emperor on
his yacht, attended a luncheon at Windsor Castle after the
burial of Edward VII of England, given a million dollars to
causes in which he believed, and owned a private yacht in
which he cruised the oceans.   A powerful man in a stirring
world!

After brief schooling in America, he continued his
education in Europe where he acquired a rich background in
history, art and literature.   There the idea of Morgan, the
collector, began to emerge.   As a fourteen-year-old, he collected fragments of stained glass, bits of which are now in-

corporated in the windows of the West Room. An autograph
of Millard Fillmore led to a lifelong interest in autographs
and documents. In the present collection are autographs and
letters of 34 presidents, including a letter of congratulation
from President Kennedy in which he wrote, "An irreplaceable
collection, beautifully housed, which began as a gift and
creation of one man, and is today a cherished public possession. "

In Rome, on a grand tour of Europe as a schoolboy,
young Morgan purchased his first art objects: a mosaic picture, an Etruscan brooch, a coral necklace and a lava ink
stand. A most careful accounting was made of every penny
spent: the largest sum, $235.50, for an oriental alabaster
vase; the smallest, 20¢, for a packing box. Fifty years later, Mr. Morgan may have smiled when he was offered the
Strozzi Palace for three million francs, and turned it down.
A visit to the library of the Duke of Devonshire in England,
where young Morgan saw a letter written by Mary, Queen of
Scots, may well have been the final catalyst in his desire to
collect.

However, at the age of twenty Mr. Morgan returned
to America and began a business career as a junior ac-
countant in a bank. Thirty years later the House of Morgan
became the mighty symbol of American "big business. "

Then, on a magnificent scale, he began to collect.
No one could believe that any one collector could buy as ex-
tensively as he did. There was scarcely an art dealer who
did not approach him. Book dealers brought him their rare
"finds. " They pursued him relentlessly at home, in hotels
and aboard his yacht. The story is told that art dealers
actually attended a "school, " learning how to approach Mr.
Morgan. Part of the instruction was in games which Mr.
Morgan enjoyed, a rather ridiculous procedure. Dealers,
however, insisted that Mr. Morgan scarcely glanced at their
art objects, but rather, testing their reliability, looked deep
into their eyes.

One unusual piece after another was purchased by Mr.
Morgan: the Mazarin tapestry; fragments from Trajan's Roman Forum; alabaster reliefs from the palace of Assurbanipal
of Ninevah; ornaments worn by barbarians after the fall of
Rome.

Mr. Morgan loved enamels, gold ornaments and jewels.

These he collected with abandon, but the paintings he purchased were perhaps his chief delight.   Many of these famous
paintings hang in museums in New York City, but one of his
favorite pictures, Portrait of a Man with a Pink by Memling,
adorns the wall of his study.

The range of his collecting was staggering.   He moved
from interest to interest.   When he had attained the best in
a field, he promptly abandoned it: "I have done with Greek
antiquities, I am at the Egyptian."   Thwarted in the purchase
of manuscripts of Lord Byron, the English poet, Mr. Morgan
stated, "I want them.   Therefore I engaged a man, gave him
a letter of credit, and told him to go to Greece and live [there]
until he had gotten those manuscripts."

At times he became overzealous in his passion for collecting.   However, on one occasion when he learned that a
beautifully embroidered cope, which he had purchased, had
been stolen from a cathedral in Italy, he promptly returned
it to the Italian government.

The last purchases made by Mr. Morgan were incunabula and illuminated manuscripts.   The sumptuous jeweled
binding of the 9th century Lindau Gospels; the Missal of Ab-
bott Berthold splendidly bound in silver gilt and a choir book;
an Antiphon, richly illuminated, are but a sampling of the
most perfect collection of illuminated manuscripts in America.
Housed in beauty and clothed in beauty, these manuscripts
reflect Mr. Morgan's devotion to the fine arts.

The Collections

The largest collection of incunabula in the world is in
Munich, Germany.   But the Morgan Library rightly prides
itself that among the nearly 2,000 incunabula it owns are
many rare items: one of the four known copies of the Constance Missal believed to have been printed by Gutenberg;
two Gutenberg Bibles, one on paper, one on vellum; Columbus's account of his voyage to the New World, printed in
Rome in 1493; the Mainz Psalter for which Mr. Morgan paid
the highest price ever known for a printed book; four very
rare Caxton's, one of them the only surviving copy of the
first edition of Malory's Morte d'Arthur, the unforgettable
story of the flashing sword, Excalibur, rising from the sea
to be grasped by the hand of the mighty Arthur.

Sharing in the august company are the hand-written manuscripts of the literary works of distinguished authors-- a collection impossible to duplicate. When he gave a holograph of Pudd'nhead Wilson to the Morgan, Mark Twain remarked that one of his high ambitions was gratified. He now stood with Burns, Scott, Keats, Shelley, Kipling, Poe and Thoreau. These drafts, criss-crossed with word changes and marginal notes, demonstrate the awesome labor of the author at work. It is a new experience for young people to see "Scrooge" in Dickens' handwriting in the manuscript of the Christmas Carol; to decipher the fable of The Fox and the Grapes in the earliest known manuscript of Aesop, and to admire the delicacy of the original illustration of Puss in Boots in the 1695 edition of Perrault's fairy tales, titled Mother Goose.

The treasures of the Morgan Library are available to scholars who are welcomed and graciously served whether their interest be in an account of the trial of Joan of Arc or a wedding picture of Martin Luther and his wife.

When Mr. Morgan died in 1913, the Times of London valued his art holdings at $60,000,000. His son, J. P. Morgan, continued for twenty years to enrich the collection. But the Library stands as a memorial to Pierpont Morgan, dedicated to the enlightenment and pleasure of the people. It is a calm and quiet oasis in a frantic modern world, a "thing of beauty."

THINK ABOUT THIS CHAPTER

In hundreds of rare collections around the world, books and manuscripts are preserved as monuments to man's artistic achievements. The collections mentioned in this chapter, the British Museum, the Folger Shakespeare Library, Bibliotheca Vaticanus and the Pierpont Morgan Library, are merely a beginning in a lifetime of journeys to other magnificent libraries and museums.

What do these rare and beautiful collections mean to you?

What are we building as shrines for the future--enormous sports complexes, the tallest buildings known to man, huge shopping centers?

Thousands of years from now will archeologists ponder over the remnants of our culture and attempt to recreate our civilization from the ruins of a capital city, a university library or a Disney World? What will they decipher from masses of decayed film, tapes, paperbacks and political documents? What do you imagine will be their interpretation of the world we live in?

Thank about this chapter.

A CHECK LIST

Listed below are 15 "persons, places and things" connected with the libraries described in this chapter: the British Museum, the Folger Shakespeare Library, Bibliotheca Vaticanus and the Pierpont Morgan Library.

Can you identify the library with which each item is associated?

The Library

1. The Rosetta Stone   1. _____

2. A statue of Puck   2. _____

3. Sir Anthony Panizzi   3. _____

4. A copy of <u>Hamlet</u> in Spanish   4. _____

5. The manuscript of Dicken's
    Christmas Carol   5. _____

6. The palimpsest of Cicero's
    <u>De Republica</u>   6. _____

7. The Diamond Sutra   7. _____

8. A jeweled binding   8. _____

9. Platina   9. _____

10. A great circular reading room   10. _____

11. Sir Robert Cotton   11. _____

12. A model of a theatre in Shake-
    speare's time   12. _____

13. The manuscripts copied in the
    old monastery at Bobbio   13. _____

14. Rolls of papyrus buried at Hercu-
     laneum when Mt. Vesuvius erupted   14. _____

15. An illuminated Psalter (Psalms),
     once belonging to Queen Mary   15. _____

FURTHER READING

Adams, Frederick B.   An Introduction to the Pierpont Mor-
     gan Library.   New York: The Library, © 1964.
          A delightful booklet about a library that has grown
from a few autographs and a piece of stained glass to a
"national asset whose value cannot be measured in mere dollars." Generously illustrated with photographs.

          The above item is listed as a sample of available
materials (largely pamphlets) on the distinguished libraries
visited in this chapter.   It is suggested that you write to
these libraries and museums, and others if you choose, inquiring as to publications relating to their history and holdings.

Addresses

The Pierpont Morgan Library
33 East 36th Street
New York, New York   10016

The Folger Shakespeare Library
Capitol Hill
Washington, D. C.

The Vatican Library
The State of Vatican City
Italy

The British Museum
Great Russell Street
London, WC1 England

Chapter 9

BOOK COLLECTING, AN AVOCATION

"And we shall not cease from exploration
And the end of all our exploring
Will be to arrive where we started
And know the place for the first time."
                                    --T. S. Eliot

The year was 1926, the place the Anderson Galleries
in New York City, the object one of the most beautiful books
ever printed by movable type, the Gutenberg Bible.   The
superb Melk copy was to be sold at auction.   A rare book,
indeed, as only 47 copies of the Gutenberg Bible were known
to the book world, and many of these precious volumes were
already safely housed in museums and libraries.   Who would
bid for this copy?   How high the price?

Down came the auctioneer's hammer.   Sold to Dr.
Rosenbach, a famous book dealer, for $106,000.   The same
day Dr. Rosenbach sold the precious Bible to Mrs. Harkness,
who gave it to Yale University where it is on display in the
entrance hall of the Harkness Library.   Lying open in a plain
glass case, the glorious book is a treasure beyond price.

Today a book collector will pay a half million dollars
for a rare item, especially if he is afflicted with bibliomania,
a disease whose symptoms may be alleviated only by the
ownership of greatly desired and unusual books--an only known
copy, all the books written by one author, or even a complete
set of Superman comic books.   In time and with care one
may become a "scholar in books."   But a dedicated book collector seldom recovers from bibliomania.

WHY COLLECT

Dozens of reasons might be given for collecting books and manuscripts. Let's consider those reasons important to an amateur collector.

As you gain a knowledge of the long history of the book, from the rude scratchings on rocks to the beautifully printed and illustrated modern book, you recognize a parallel with the development of man himself, as he searched for individual expression, dignity, and the meaning of things greater than himself. The book marched beside him. The poet Archibald MacLeish claims that the book was a greater invention than the wheel. He may well be right.

If you are convinced that books are sources of satisfaction for an insatiable curiosity, a compulsion "to find the facts, face the fact and follow the facts," whether they be concerned with a space journey to Mars, the game and play of chess, or the name of a white-capped bird lighting at a back yard feeder, then you have a second reason for pursuing the book collecting game.

A strong desire to avoid a "Where-did-you-go?--Out--What-did-you-do?--Nothing" attitude may well result in an effort to extend your interests, be it the collecting of stamps, hockey pucks hit over the glass by Esposito, the care and feeding of long-haired rabbits or the reading of biographies of General Patton.

One day you may copy into a battered notebook a line or two of poetry or a remembered phrase that hits you like a blow in your mind and heart. You have begun word collecting, and it is no giant step from word collecting to book collecting.

Surround yourself with books--paperbacks or volumes in hard covers. As your interests grow, so grows your collection. Book collecting has now begun for you.

STEPS FOR THE COLLECTOR

Remember that you make the decision to play the game depending largely on your interest in a particular subject, be

it road maps or a facsimile* of a wondrous Book of
Hours.

Step 1 - Visit a large book store. Browse. Ask
questions. Examine books relating to your interest. You
may find a paperback on magicians or a pamphlet on witch's
covens, if the black arts are your particular interest. Buy
a book. Look for a bin of books on sale. Perhaps that
dusty, little book on werewolves will catch your attention.

Step 2 - Ask your librarian for a list of booksellers
dealing in rare and unusual books. Send for their catalogs.
Then, with pencil in hand, you can day-dream delightfully.
Check the items you might like to own. Build a shelf of
these catalogs. Study carefully the descriptions of the books
for sale, especially the abbreviations used. Write to a book
dealer inquiring about books in your special sphere of interest. He will keep in touch with you if he realizes that your
requests are more than idle curiosity.

Step 3 - Read the amusing and sometimes enigmatic
experiences of collectors and book dealers. Astute and clever in the rare book trade, Dr. Rosenbach spent his life a-
mong books and enjoyed every minute of it. You might enjoy a recounting of his experiences in A Book Hunter's Holi-
day.

The author remembers with pleasure a visit to Dr.
Rosenbach's New York book rooms, including a welcome by
the parrot at the foot of the stairway. This day Dr. Rosenbach was much distressed. A visitor, ecstatic at seeing a
first edition of Walt Whitman's Leaves of Grass, had in his
excitement dropped the book and broken the binding. Down
went the value of the book as a collector's item.

Step 4 - Write to other book collectors. Contacts
with other collectors whose interests are similar to yours
are pleasant and easily made by checking classified advertise-
ments in literary magazines. Note the following request that
appeared recently in one of these magazines:

"Looking for an answer. Was Jack London's To Build
a Fire published as a separate? Correspondence on same
welcomed. Write P.O. Box 251, Ossian Hills, N.Y."

---

*A facsimile is an exact reproduction or copy.

Or if you are collecting Horatio Algers, a series of long ago rags-to-riches books for boys, write Dr. Leslie Poste* and inquire as to other collectors of Alger books. Exchange ideas. You are coming down with bibliomania.

Step 5 - Attend a book auction at a gallery or at a book dealer's. At a book auction there is usually a solemn stillness. Listen to the auctioneer and you will learn much about books. Go early to the auction room and examine the items for sale. Watch the book dealers as they bid silently by raising a finger or pulling an ear. The auctioneer recognizes these secret maneuvers.

Step 6 - Store your collection carefully. Know it from cover to cover--text, binding, end papers, title page, date of publication, copyright date, appendices, book jacket, type design, dedication, paper and illustration.

You may be quite sure you are a collector if you appreciate this story about a young and eminent book collector, Harry Widener. Mr. Widener had been on a book buying expedition in England and was to return home on the Titanic, little knowing that it was the ship's final voyage. Mr. Widener was overjoyed that at long last he had found the book he so greatly desired, a second edition of Bacon's Essays, as rare and scarce as a first edition. Shortly before boarding ship, he put the precious book in his coat pocket and laughingly said, "If there is a shipwreck, little Bacon and I will go down together." They did.

WHAT TO COLLECT

Many a rare volume in libraries and museums, and many a collection of beloved books in homes, "just grew" like Topsy. What do people collect? A number of examples may be recounted: six cook books, then hundreds lining a kitchen wall; first editions of the Rex Stout mysteries featuring the fat, erudite Nero Wolfe; dime novels read secretly as a child up in the hay mow; old auction bills listing pot-bellied stoves and hay tedders, meaningful to a country boy in years gone by; fore-edge paintings revealed by fanning back the front edges of the book pages; maps, old and new,

*Dr. Leslie Poste, Lakeville Rd., Geneseo, N.Y. 14454.

including maps of buried treasure; theatre programs of plays
attended during a 50-year period; picture books illustrated
by Maurice Sendak, an enthusiasm engendered by Where the
Wild Things Are; or one hundred baseballs autographed by
famous players.

Americana

Many collectors delight in Americana--books or other
materials on the Civil War, silver, old letters and documents,
pictures taken on the moon, accounts of drilling for oil in
Pennsylvania.

Local History. Since it is wise to limit a collection
of Americana to one era, let us consider local history.
Usually there is a county historian or a County Historical
Society to give you direction. Investigate old plank roads or
account books of tavern keepers during stage coach days,
listing dinner and overnight lodging for 39 cents. The origin
of place names such as Podunk or Poge's Hole are fun to
pursue. If your home town was once Indian country you will
have heard myths and legends about Indian burial grounds,
Indian trails and treaties. Was it in your country that Paul
Bunyan hitched Babe, the Blue Ox, to a crooked river and
pulled it straight? Pecos Bill was raised by the coyotes.
Did he lasso a cyclone in your hills? Have you listened to
the story of Mary Jamieson, the "White Woman of the Gene-
see," who lived for many years with the Indians, an Indian
captive?

Legends of the Indians explaining to their satisfaction
the unexplainable in nature are a part of our heritage. Many
of these legends are as delightful as the one that follows:

> The East Wind looking out from his cave one morn-
> ing spied far to the west a beautiful maiden. All
> day he watched her moving in the breezes on the
> plain, her golden hair shining in the sun. The
> East Wind rose early the next day that he might
> again watch this golden-haired maiden. Alas!
> Her hair had turned white. The East Wind was so
> sad that he sighed deeply three times. And the
> maiden disappeared.

The Frontier. To young readers the frontier may
mean space exploration or the miracles of electronics, but

to many book collectors the frontier means owning every biography of the men who drove the covered wagons into new
country; and the men and women who, in a cruel winter,
tried to struggle over the Donner Pass, the last barrier of
the Continental Divide, and turned to cannibalism to survive.

Jesse James, Wild Bill Hickok and Billy the Kid, who
at twenty-one years of age had 21 notches on his gun, may
represent an ugly feature of American life. However, books
and memorabilia concerning these authors and "bad men" delight collectors.

Railroads. Railroad buffs will travel far to take a
last ride on the old "B and L line," or a first ride on a 105
m. p. h. super rocket. Timetables, a pot-bellied stove from
the waiting room of a rural depot, a bell from an old loco-
motive, or a replica of the "golden spike" may well serve as
an initial impetus to collecting material on American railroads.

Recognized as a most distinguished collector of Americana and of rare editions of English literary works, Henry E.
Huntington built in San Marino, California a beautiful marble
Library and Art Gallery. In the surrounding gardens were
planted specimens of every known tree and shrub native to
North America. A mecca for the artist who wishes to see
the original painting of the Blue Boy; a student who desires
to annotate an obscure line of English poetry; an historian
bent on verifying a "saying" of Benjamin Franklin in the
manuscript of his Autobiography, the library also holds great
interest for the collector of rare items on railroads--the
source of Mr. Huntington's wealth.

Wars. Of considerable interest to collectors is material on wars in which the United States has been involved,
especially World War I and World War II. Relics, letters,
campaign maps, diaries, biographies and memoirs of generals
and foot soldiers are eagerly sought. A collector who is
known to the author, motivated by his ownership of a pair of
knitted socks worn by a soldier in the front line trenches of
World War I, built a splendid library on trench warfare. A
book bound in human skin influenced the collecting of books in
extraordinary bindings. An interest, humble or bizarre, may
open a new world for you.

Documents and Newspapers. Documents which are
cherished as the touchstones of our democracy--the Declaration of Independence and the Constitution--are on display at

the National Archives, Washington, D.C.   We all own them.
But you may have in your family an historic deed of a government land grant, or of a cobblestone house built long ago; a
bundle of letters from a soldier in Vietnam or a letter written by your great, great grandfather relating the inconvenience
of westward train travel without toilets.   These letters, documents and keepsakes, a part of a family tradition, may lead
to a valuable collection of Americana.

        The amateur collector is often over-enthusiastic about
"gold in your attic."   On one occasion an attic trunk held a
real treasure.   Several copies of the Massachusetts Spy, a
newspaper that staunchly defended the ideals of freedom in
Colonial America, were found in an old, battered trunk and
became a nucleus of a rare collection of newspapers.   Newspapers, old and new, are not only recorded history, but
history as it happens.   At a moment in time the past, present and future are one.   A newspaper dated November 11,
1919, with PEACE blazoned across the front page, reporting
the end of World War I; a banner head setting forth the
Emancipation Proclamation on September 23, 1862; or an issue of a Chicago daily bearing the headline Dewey Defeats
Truman, may become the prized possession of a museum, a
part of the contents of a time capsule or the joy of a collector's heart.

        Children's Books.   Very possibly on your book shelves
are copies of the A. A. Milne books, neatly boxed, a gift
from a book-loving aunt.   Standing beside the Milne titles
may be several tales by Beatrix Potter with delightful illustrations of rabbits, squirrels and rats busily engaged in carrying
out their life styles.   A shelf may hold piles of comic books.
Have you kept all published copies of Superman?   The author
knows of an astute mother who bought two copies of the Superman comics, one for her son to read and "trade," the
other to preserve as a rare item along with many copies of
the "big-little" books.   In time this may prove to be a highly
profitable venture.   Do your shelves also hold copies of the
Newbery and Caldecott Award books--The Island of the Blue
Dolphin or N. C. Higgins, the Great?

        Here is the beginning of a collection of children's
books.   You may never rival the rare children's books collected by Dr. Rosenbach, nor may you ever own a copy of
the New England Primer, a rare piece of Americana.   It
was a school book and literally "used up."   Illustrated with
crude woodcuts, it included the famous alphabet--"In Adams

fall we sinned all"; the Lord's Prayer; a Cathechism and a debate between Christ and the Devil.   For recreational reading a child in Colonial New England might choose a book on manners, entreating him not to spit, cough or blow his nose at table, or a book recounting the joyful deaths of good boys and girls.   These early books, meagre in content and ugly in form when compared with the thousands of modern children's books published each year, books gay with color and diverse in content, present a social history of child life.   Children's books are a fascinating field for the amateur collector.

Autographs

Early in the 1900s when autograph collecting was the fashion in Victorian England, signatures were heedlessly clipped from letters as samples of the handwriting of famous people.   With the popularity of motion picture "stars" came another fad for collecting.   The autograph hound was born. Crowds gather around public idols and half-heroes to obtain their signatures.

Book stores often give author autograph parties. Guests treasure a book signed by an author if there has been pleasant communication between the author and the guest.   An admirer of the poems of Robert Frost finds his autographed copy has increased in personal as well as monetary value, especially if Mr. Frost has signed his name under the words --"And miles to go before I sleep. "

At Book Fairs distinguished authors of books for children and young people prove to be delightful visitors.   Their talks to audiences about the fun and the dedicated labor in the creation of a book, their conversations with individuals and their signatures on books make a terrific impact on the thousands of young people at a Fair.   Held dear will be a copy of Ferdinand with "For Susan - Munro Leaf, " or "Walter Farley" written across the title page of the Black Stallion.

Armstrong Sperry charmed the children at the Tampa, Florida, Book Fair as he told them of his experiences in writing Call It Courage and sang the chants of the Polynesian people.   Following the program the children crowded around the table to buy Call It Courage and to have it autographed by Mr. Sperry.   An adult onlooker noticed one small boy going frantically through his pockets, counting his money.   A stricken look came over his face.   He lacked 16 cents to buy

the book. Very quietly the necessary 16 cents was slipped
into his hand and a happy boy owned the book. Mr. Sperry,
with a whispered word from the adult, wrote on the title page
a special message for the boy.

The autograph can be an intimate and exciting contact
between the collector and a distinguished and gracious person, but a collector should be certain that his prized autograph is not the product of an "autograph mill," as was the
case with the signature of Franklin Delano Roosevelt.

The most coveted autographs are those of the signers
of the Declaration of Independence. Only 33 complete sets
of signatures can be assembled. Button Gwinnett, a member
of the Continental Congress, was wary with his signature.
A Button Gwinnett letter is worth $100,000 in the book mar-
ket today.

The Bible

Dr. Rosenbach tells us that family Bibles were frequently brought to him with the idea that since they were old,
they must be rare and valuable. The disappointed owners
took them home, having learned that a Bible as a collector's
item is of little value unless it was printed between 1455 and
1476.

However, there are Bible oddities which sometimes intrigue collectors. Most common are: the shirt pocket Bible
that stopped a bullet on a battlefield; the Breeches Bible, so
named because the 7th verse of the 3rd chapter of Genesis
reads, "they sewed fig leaves together and made themselves
breeches"; the Vinegar Bible with the misprint of the word
vinegar for vineyard in the Parable; the Wicked Bible which
omits the 7th Commandment, and miniature Bibles, some no
larger than a postage stamp.

Banned Books

Through the ages books have been censored, banned
and burned; booksellers jailed and authors exiled for sub-
versive statements. Heresy, treason and obscenity have been
charged by governments and by the church.

Collections of banned books are not unusual. A list

of banned books may be found in a book titled <u>Banned Books,</u>
which gives informal notes indicating the variety of reasons
for books being included. *

You may be surprised to know that the Bible has been
banned many times.   Tyndale's translation of the New Testament was burned publicly by order of the church.   Later,
Tyndale was burned at the stake for his heresy.   Shakespeare's
<u>Merchant of Venice</u> was censored in a High School in New
York State; Mark Twain's <u>Tom Sawyer</u> banned in Russia;
<u>Huckleberry Finn</u> discarded as trash by a New England Pub-
lic Library; <u>Little Black Sambo</u> taken off library shelves because of an implied racial slur; and in East Berlin, Germany,
the Mickey Mouse comics were banished because Mickey was
a rebel.

In the Square in front of the University of Berlin in
1933, the Nazis burned 35,000 books because their authors
were Jewish.   In the bonfire were books by Helen Keller,
Jack London, Ernest Hemingway and Sigmund Freud!

"The world is so full of a number of things," says
Lewis Carroll.   You, too may be saying, "Enough! I've
read of such numbers of things to collect that I scarcely
know where to begin."   True, but your best incentive for
collecting is to proceed wherever your own keen interest
leads you.

Association Copies

By definition, an association copy is a book identified
with a unique event, with its ownership by a famous man or
woman, or by an unusual incident relating to the book.   The
collecting of association copies can begin at home with the
family Bible recording births and deaths of generations; a
gift book treasured because a friend wrote a secret message
in it; a "prize" book given for the highest scholastic rating
in Science, or a Prayer Book presented to an altar boy for
faithful service.   The author has a copy of the <u>Wide, Wide
World,</u> on the fly-leaf of which is written, "In memory of
summer hours we spent in the sweet apple tree reading and
re-reading this book."

*Haight, Anne Lyon.   <u>Banned Books.</u>   2nd ed. , rev. and enl.
New York: Bowker, 1955.

Association copies may surround a collector, but there
are certain ones he can only dream of owning: the books
Abe Lincoln read by firelight; the volume of Keats' poems,
opened to the Eve of St. Agnes, found in Shelley's coat pocket
when his body was washed ashore; a copy of the Book of
Common Prayer being discussed by the Rector on the day that
an old Scotch woman threw her prayer stool at him; the school
books of the recently exiled author, Alexander Solzhenitsyn;
books read by Mary, Queen of Scots, while in prison awaiting
the headsman's axe. A collector may well spend a lifetime
among association copies.

Forgeries

As rare books become rarer and prices rise, the
temptation to reproduce valuable books grows. Many collectors are at first bedazzled by these fakes and then duped.
A forger of books and manuscripts must be clever and
knowledgeable; the handwriting must be copied exactly or the
type cut to perfection. The greatest danger to the forger
lies in the choice of paper, as many forgeries have thus been
uncovered. In time a forger is usually discovered. Here
are the stories of two famous forgeries.

Fakes and Forgeries. The Ireland forgeries are so
well known that collectors will buy forgeries of the forgeries.
The father of William Henry Ireland was a London engraver
who believed Shakespeare to be the greatest author who ever
lived. Young Ireland longed to find a piece of Shakespear-
eana--a letter, an autograph, or an act of a play to present
to his father. Apprenticed as a clerk in a lawyer's cham-
bers, young Ireland found among the old legal documents a
roll of unused parchment. On it he copied a lease signed by
Shakespeare and took it home to his ecstatic father. From
then on young Ireland continued to "discover" rare Shakespearean items: a love letter to Ann Hathaway; a lock of
Shakespeare's hair; a manuscript of King Lear and, for good
measure, pages of Hamlet. It was before these manuscripts
that the biographer, Boswell, is said to have knelt in reverence. Then young Ireland surprised his father with the
manuscript of a hitherto unknown play by Shakespeare. Sus-
picious scholars severely questioned this latest forgery. Ireland confessed.

There have been several Columbus "fakes." One concerns a log book Columbus kept during his first voyage. On

his return voyage to Spain, a vast storm arose. Fearing
that his ship might sink, Columbus placed in a wooden chest
a record of his New World discoveries and threw the chest
overboard. However, the ship rode out the storm, and Columbus received the homage of King Ferdinand and Queen
Isabella. Four hundred years later a Welsh sailor wrote to
a London publisher that, while trawling, he had pulled into
his net a wooden box. In it was an old log book. The publisher was gullible and issued My Secrete Log Boke, written
by Christopher Columbus. The wooden box onto which shells
and barnacles had been glued was exhibited along with the
Log Boke. No one was hoodwinked by this comic hoax.

GUIDELINES FOR IDENTIFYING A RARE BOOK

Several times in this chapter the term "a rare book"
has been used to characterize a collector's item. What makes
a book rare?

A rare book is an "important, desirable, hard-to-get
book." A book is important if it has great literary merit--
a play by Shakespeare; if it has historical significance--the
Federalist Papers in which were set forth the principles of
American democracy; or, if by a pronounced thesis it changed
the minds and hearts of a nation, as did Mein Kampf. A
book becomes a hard-to-get book when a frustrated collector
desires a particular edition as a self-monument and searches
in vain for a copy in the book market.

What makes a book rare? A quick answer is: beauty,
binding, scarcity, demand, mint condition and a first edition.
Very important to a book collector are these characteristics,
so important that a brief review of each is essential for the
amateur collector. Let's consider them one by one.

Beauty. Today, the large, expensive "non-book" illustrated with a profusion of color photographs printed on
high gloss paper may be considered a beautiful book. Some
of them are. Beauty in a book, however, lies in its handmade paper with delicate chain lines and distinctive watermark;
in fine printing easily read and perfectly balanced on the page;
in illustration--engravings, woodcuts, pictorial maps, rubrics,
initial letters, well designed head and tail pieces artistically
one with the content of the book.

Binding. In the days of the great patrons of art, a
book binder dressed his patron's books in crimson velvet,
in enamels, embroidered designs, jewels, family crests,
bosses and clasps of gold and silver. When expertly tanned
leathers--calf, sheep, doe, pig, seal, goat, kangaroo--came
into use, the binder's tools were few and simple. The leather was stamped in blind (without gold) or with gold laid on
in repeated designs of sprays of flowers, grains, foliage,
vases, garlands, geometric designs.

Binders created handsome covers for royalty. The
books of Francis I, King of France, were embellished with
a golden F surmounted by a golden crown. Diane de Poitiers
used as a cover design on her magnificently bound books the
bow, arrows and crescent, a "play" on her name, Diana,
Goddess of the Chase. After she became the mistress of
Henri II of France, she added an H to her monogram and
made free use of the royal fleur-de-lis. Henri III forbade
the French binders to use more than four diamonds on a
book cover lest the bindings of his own books be surpassed.

Books in rare bindings may often be seen on exhibition
in museums and libraries and an informed visitor looks for
a Grolier, a Roger Payne or a T. Cobden-Sanderson binding.
Each has its own style. Grolier used a geometric design in
gold, usually on olive-green morocco, the cover bearing the
motto, Grolierii et Amicorum. Roger Payne's bindings are
simple and elegant with much attention to the decoration of
the spine of the book. The modern English binder, T. Cobden-Sanderson, expresses in his artistic floral designs the
idea of growth from root to bud to blossom.

As you become familiar with binding styles you may
enjoy imagining a distinctive style for your own books--per-
haps a dark red morocco with gold on the spine and the family coat of arms on the cover, or a white pigskin with a
favorite flower stamped in gold. Unfortunately, professional
binders today are few and the cost is so high that this fancy
must be reserved for wealthy collectors.

Scarcity. As libraries and museums have built their
collections of rare books, fewer have become available to
collectors. Moreover, books are fragile. Fire, flood, war,
children, dust and disease have taken their toll. Hundreds
of books were destroyed in London after the Great Plague.
A volume of the Federalist Papers (1788) served as a door-
stop. A copy of Venus and Adonis by Shakespeare provided

the target in an archery contest.   A book can be literally
read to pieces.   Of the 1600 printed copies of the Bay Psalm
Book only eleven are in existence.

The whim of an author is yet another factor in scarcity.   Robert Frost, the poet, had printed but two copies of
his first book of poems, Twilight.   One copy he destroyed.
The second copy he gave to his wife.   If you were a collector bent on securing first editions of every book written by
one author, it would be impossible to gather a complete set
of first editions of Robert Frost's poems.   The rare copy belonging to his wife was sold years ago for $3,500.   One
satisfied collector!

Mint Condition.   The rare book must usually be in
mint condition--as "shining" as a newly minted penny, a clean
copy as good as new.   The collector is likely to ask: Is the
book in its original binding?   Is the spine of the book un-
damaged, with no sign of having been pulled off the shelf by
the top of the spine, a practice common to 90 per cent of
book users?   Are there traces of bookworms cut into the
paper?   A bookworm cares not whether a book costs 10 cents
or $1000.   Is the paper stained or foxed?   Are the end
papers clean?   Is there an absence of marginal notes and
underlined words?

Printed reviews pasted on the inside cover or scrib-
bling of personal comments detract from the value of the book
unless these comments have been made by a famous author or
critic.   An amusing story is told of a collector who was hor-
rified at a sentence or two written on the flyleaf of a book.
He refused to buy the book because it was not in mint condition.   Too late came the realization that the initials RWE
signed at the end of a sentence were those of Ralph Waldo
Emerson, American philosopher and essayist.   The book was
a rare association copy.

A book in mint condition will often have uncut pages.
If an implement is used to cut joined pages, at that instant
the value of the book is lessened.   Original dust wrappers,
like the dull grey paper jackets on the first edition of John
Galsworthy's novels, are greatly desired by the collector.
Careful handling of books, rare or not, is essential for maintaining them in mint condition.

First Editions.   It is in the quest for first editions
that the collector becomes a bibliomaniac.   The story is told

of a conversation between a visitor to a country estate and
the owner. "What a fine stand of old elms," gushed the
visitor. "If they could speak, what would they say?"
"Hurumph," replied the host, "they would say we are oaks."
What is a first edition--an elm, an oak, or neither? There
is no absolute answer.

By definition a first edition is the first appearance of
a written work in book form. A collector, insistent that he
wants only a first edition, or doubtful that he has one, may
depend on the following criteria: a minute centimeter-by-
centimeter comparison of his book with a known first edition;
the validation of a common copyright date and publishing date;
an understanding of a secret code used by publishing houses
to signify a first edition, such as the letter A under the copyright date, and the expectation that the words, First Edition,
printed on the title pages are reliable.

A criterion which challenges and delights a collector
in search of an authentic first edition is known as Points--
a word used by bibliographers to designate a change in the
form or content of the book after a first printing.

Points may consist of a change in the weight of the
paper; an alteration in type faces; a deviation in the binding
of the book or errors in the text. Once the presses are
stopped and a correction is made, the book is no longer a
first edition.

Entertaining comments about Points circulate in the
rare book market. The dedication in Ben Hur by General
Lew Wallace read: "To the wife of my youth." Shortly after
the release of the novel, General Wallace received letters
of sympathy at the death of his wife. Mrs. Wallace was
alive and well. The presses were stopped and added to the
dedication were the words, "who still abides with me." On
which dedication does the collector of a first edition insist?
In The Cloister and the Hearth by Charles Reade a sentence
reads: "the woman threw her face over her apron." To a
collector of first editions of English novels a corrected copy
has little value. A first edition of Edith Wharton's Age of
Innocence may be genuine if the wedding ceremony begins
with the burial service--"As it hath pleased Almighty God."

A bibliophile would consider these guide lines for identifying first editions over-simplified; he knows full well that
highly specialized knowledge is essential in determining a

first edition.   A chapter in <u>A Primer of Book Collecting</u>
(see Further Reading at end of this chapter) relates with
clarity and vigor the excitement in the search for first editions.   The chapter begins, "It is the collector's business
to know what he wants."

A MULTIPLE CHOICE SUMMARY

Check the box opposite the correct statement.

1.   Which book listed below, has been the most widely banned
     around the world?

     ☐   <u>Mein Kampf</u>

     ☐   <u>The Bible</u>

     ☐   Einstein's <u>The Meaning of Relativity</u>

2.   How would you define <u>Americana</u> as a collector's item?

     ☐   Books printed by the House of Aldus

     ☐   Books printed by xylography

     ☐   Books dealing with life and times in America

3.   What is an association copy?

     ☐   A book issued by a popular association or society
         such as the <u>National Geographic Society</u>

     ☐   A book that at one time belonged to a famous per-
         son or was connected with a special event

     ☐   A book recommended by the National Book Associa-
         tion

4.   The Melk copy of the Gutenberg Bible purchased by Mrs.
     Harkness is considered to be the most perfect copy in
     America.   Where is it housed?

     ☐   Library of Congress

☐ Yale University Library

☐ New York Public Library

5. Why is it almost impossible for a collector today to own a complete set of autographs of the signers of the Declaration of Independence?

☐ There are but a few autographs of Thomas Jefferson available

☐ There are but a few autographs of John Hancock available

☐ There are but a few autographs of Button Gwinnett available

6. Of the men mentioned below only one was a famous binder of books.   Which one?

☐ Thomas B. Hart

☐ Grolier

☐ Caxton

7. Why did Dr. Rosenbach, the famous book dealer, pay a huge sum to obtain the Ireland forgeries?

☐ Because they were very cleverly done

☐ Because they might be considered as Shakespeareana

☐ Because they were in beautiful bindings

8. What is the most certain way of verifying that your favorite book is a first edition?

☐ Compare it with a known first edition

☐ Depend upon your book dealer's opinion

☐ Check the dedication in the book

9. What makes a book rare?   Two criteria are listed below. Write in two further criteria.

    '(1)   Purchase by libraries and museums, thereby taking the book out of the market and making it scarce.

    (2)   "Fashions" in book collecting. For example, collectors insist on first editions of Charles Dickens' books. Dickens is "in style."

    (3)

    (4)

10.   Considered as the most likely way to begin collecting books is that of buying books related to one's special interest, be it football or a time and space theory.

    What might you consider as Step 2? _____

_____

    Step 3? _____

_____

    Begin book collecting with your special interest. Buy a book on the subject. Buy another. Fill a shelf or two. Review the guidelines for book collecting in this chapter. If you then take the next step, you will have an avocation that may well lead to a lifetime of learning and pleasure.

FURTHER READING

Bradley, Van Allen. Gold in Your Attic. New York: Fleet, 1958.
    You may think you have a rare book at home worth half a king's ransom, only to find that it is of no value. Or you may have a treasure in the bookcase that you do not recognize. Gold in Your Attic may help you to decide what is valuable.

Newton, Alfred Edward. This Book-Collecting Game. Boston: Little, Brown, 1928.
    Some time ago, the rare books, original drawings, autographed letters and manuscripts collected by Mr. Newton, a gentleman and a scholar, were offered for sale at the Parke-Bernet galleries in New York City. Mr. Newton wanted oth-

ers to share his treasures after his death.   On each page of
This Book-Collecting Game one glimpses the meaning of a
genuine love of books.

Rosenbach, Abraham S. W.   Books and Bidders.   Boston:
    Little, Brown, 1927.
        Here are the amazing adventures of a book collector
who, from his early days in the book shop of his Uncle Moses
in Philadelphia, became the owner of a fabulous library near
Fifth Avenue, New York City.   Collectors came to buy items
--a professor for a first edition, or a robber baron for an
illuminated manuscript.   Entertaining reading.

Winterich, John T. and Randall, D. A.   The Primer of Book
    Collecting.   3d rev. ed.   New York: Crown, 1966.
        The lure of the chase.   Plenty of practical advice on
what to buy in the rare book market place.   Might be enjoyed
as a "how to" book on book collecting.

INDEX

Abbreviations, manuscripts, 68
Acrophonic principle, 8, 13
Aldus Manutius see Printers, early
Alexandrian library, arrangement, 49; collection, 48; destruc-
    tion, 50; librarians, 49; organization, 48-49
Alphabet, pictograph, 6-8; ideogram, 8; letter sound, 9;
    phonogram, 8-9; syllabic sound, 9
Americana, 154-157
Aristotle, library of, 47
Armarius, monastic librarian, 66-67, 98-99
Association copies, 159-160
Assurbanipal, library of, 39-42
Autographs, 157-158

Banned books, 158
Bibles, 42-line, 113; 36-line, 114; Eliot's Indian translation,
    123; Plantin's polygot, 120; see also Book collecting
Block books, 111
Bodleian, Oxford University, arrangement and care of books,
    104-105; collections, 104-105; Humphrey, Duke of
    Gloucester library, 103-104
Bodley, Sir Thomas, 104; see also Book collectors
Book bindings, 81, 82, 101, 140, 162
Book collecting, procedures for, 151-153; selected areas of
    interest, 153-161; see also Americana, Association copies,
    Autographs, Banned books, Bibles, Forgeries
Book collectors; Thomas Bodley, 104; Richard du Bury, 100;
    Robert Cotton, 132; Henry Clay Folger, 137-138; Robert
    Harley, 132; Humphrey, Duke of Gloucester, 103; Henry
    E. Huntington, 155; Medici family, 101-102; Pierpont
    Morgan, 144-146; Abraham S. W. Rosenbach, 152, 156,
    158; Hans Sloane, 132-133
Book of Kells, 77-79
Book of the Dead, 46
Book shops and booksellers, 52-99
British Museum, London, founding, 132-133; growth and
    change, 133-134; Panizzi, 133-134; treasures, 135-136